Zambia Social Science Journal Vol. 3, No. 1
(April 2012)

A publication of the Southern African Institute for Policy and Research

Zambia Social Science Journal



The *Zambia Social Science Journal* is published under the auspices of the Southern African Institute for Policy and Research. The primary objective is to publish scholarly work in the social sciences and development. Serving as a forum for argument, debate, review, reflection, and discussion, the Journal is informed by the results of relevant and rigorous research. The published papers are peer reviewed by anonymous reviewers. Final acceptance or rejection of submitted papers rests with the Editorial Board. The Editorial Board reserves the right to refuse any material for publication. The Journal is published bi-annually, with editions coming out in April and November. Subscriptions rates are available on request.

# Zambia Social Science Journal Vol. 3, No. 1 (April 2012)

Edited by

Jotham Momba

CAMBRIDGE SCHOLARS

PUBLISHING

Zambia Social Science Journal Vol. 3, No. 1 (April 2012) ,
Edited by Jotham Momba

This book first published 2014

Cambridge Scholars Publishing

12 Back Chapman Street, Newcastle upon Tyne, NE6 2XX, UK

British Library Cataloguing in Publication Data
A catalogue record for this book is available from the British Library



ISSN 2079-5521

In memory of Lawrence Michelo (1976 - 2013)

# CONTENTS

# TECHNICAL EFFICIENCY OF UGANDA'S PRIMARY SCHOOLS

BRUNO L. YAWE
MAKERERE UNIVERSITY

*This article measures the technical efficiency of Uganda's primary schools over the 1995-2009 period. Technical efficiency measures the extent to which a given school or group of schools turn the inputs at their disposal into desirable educational outputs. Ideally, we would measure desirable educational outcomes in terms of factors such as self-confidence, earning potential, and occupational mobility, but these tend to be long-term. Therefore, this study focused on more immediate educational outputs. The study demonstrates that Uganda's primary schools are technically inefficient, as none has attained an efficiency score of 100%. Nevertheless, the observed inefficiency should be interpreted cautiously, bearing in mind existing institutional and resource gaps in terms of physical and human infrastructure (e.g. classrooms, funding, toilets, and teachers). Additionally, pupil attributes should be incorporated in an efficiency analysis.*

## 1. Introduction[1]

The introduction of the Universal Primary Education (UPE) programme increased access to education in Uganda. There was a 4% increase in the number of pupils enrolled between 2008 and 2009 and a 7% increase in the number of primary schools between 2008 and 2009. The total number of classrooms also increased by 6% over the same period. However, the provision of adequate infrastructure for the children enrolled in primary schools remains a key challenge. At the national level, about one in every three pupils does not have adequate sitting and writing space (Uganda Bureau of Statistics, 2010). Although substantial resources have been directed to primary education in Uganda, there is a knowledge gap with regard to the extent to which the resources have been converted into desirable educational outputs. To bridge this gap, this article sought to measure the extent to which primary schools in Uganda were technically efficient.

The article measures the technical efficiency of Uganda's primary schools over the 1995-2009 period. Ajibefun (2008) notes that the measurement of technical efficiency is important for the following reasons: Firstly, it is an indicator of performance by which production units are evaluated. Secondly, measurement of the causes of inefficiency makes it possible to explore the sources of efficiency differentials and to eliminate the causes of inefficiency. Finally, the identification of the sources of inefficiency is essential to the institution of policies to improve performance.

The article is organised into eight sections. The next section presents previous selected studies on primary education. Section 3 describes the methodology employed. The unit of analysis, data type, sources, and sample size are presented in section 4. Empirical results are presented in section 5; whilst section 6 positions the article's findings within the body of existing knowledge. The article's conclusions are the subject matter of section 7, while the policy implications of the article are presented in section 8.

## 2. Previous Studies on Primary Education in Uganda

The economics of education has been analysed through three approaches: child development, production function, and school 'market' structure. The early childhood approach looks at the student's environment to explain the development of cognitive skills. Family background and the social environment in which a child develops, often without regard to school inputs, are the main determinants of cognitive achievement. The production function approach stresses the linkage between school inputs and cognitive achievements, whilst the education market approach focuses upon how competition in the provision of education affects the cognitive skills of students. However, elements of all three approaches affect cognitive achievement. Todd and Wolpin (2003) point out that focusing on a particular aspect to the exclusion of others requires very restrictive assumptions.

Previous studies have been undertaken with respect to Uganda's primary education. These relate to factors such as a shortage of teachers and accountability and transparency. A shortage of teachers has been cited in various studies (Ministry of Education and Sports, 2000). While student enrolment has steadily grown since the inception of UPE, the number of primary teachers has not grown at a commensurate rate to ensure the acceptable teacher-pupil ratio of 40:1.

Transparency International (2010) presented a regional overview of accountability and transparency in primary education management in seven African countries (including Uganda). The World Bank (2010) introduced the term 'quiet corruption' to indicate various types of malpractice by frontline providers (teachers, doctors, inspectors, and other government representatives) that do not involve monetary exchange. The cited behaviours include potentially observable deviations, such as absenteeism, and hard-to-observe deviations from expected conduct, such as a lower level of effort than expected or the deliberate bending of rules for personal advantage. The report notes that primary school teachers in a number of African countries (including Uganda) are not in school 15-25% of the time (absenteeism), but, additionally, a considerable fraction of those present are not found teaching (low-effort).

Nishimura et al (2009) make a comparative analysis of universal primary education in four countries, namely, Ghana, Kenya, Malawi, and Uganda, to identify common and unique themes and to examine how these seemingly similar policies are responding to the capacity and needs of each country. The results show that effective policy implementation requires considerable consultation with key stakeholders and a baseline survey that would enable systematic implementation and consideration of equity.

The leakage of resources is a key constraint to primary education in Uganda. Between 1995 and 2001, leakage of capitation grants to schools in Uganda fell from 80% to 20%. While some of this improvement may have occurred without the Public Expenditure Tracking Studies (PETS), it seems the decrease of leakage was mainly a result of the PETS and the policy changes that it triggered (UNESCO, 2004). The above demonstrates that primary education has various institutional (policy and infrastructural) challenges.

## 3. Measuring Technical Efficiency Using Data Envelopment Analysis

Farrell (1957, cited in Coelli, 1996) proposed that the efficiency of a firm consists of two components: technical efficiency, which reflects the ability of a firm to obtain maximal output from a given set of inputs, and allocative (price) efficiency, which reflects the ability of a firm to use inputs in optimal proportions, given their respective prices and the production technology. Technical efficiency was measured by means of a non-parametric Data Envelopment Analysis (DEA). A combination of technical and allocative efficiency yields a measure of total economic (overall) efficiency. In the context of education, this implies academic achievement for a given level of expenditure.

The three measures of efficiency (technical, allocative, and economic) are bounded by zero and unity. They are measured along a ray from the origin to the observed production point. They hold the relative proportions of inputs (or outputs) constant. One merit of these radial efficiency measures is that they are unit invariant. This means that changing the units of measurement does not change the value of the efficiency measure (Coelli, 1996). The final dimension of efficiency is scale efficiency. A production unit is 'scale efficient' when its size of operation is optimal. At the optimal scale, when the size of operation is either reduced or increased, its efficiency will drop. A scale efficient unit is one that operates at optimal returns to scale.

Charnes et al (1978) proposed a DEA model, which had an input-orientation and assumed Constant Returns to Scale (CRS). They specified a fractional linear programme that computes the relative efficiency of each Decision Making Unit (DMU) by comparing it to all the other observations in the sample. Their exposition proceeds as follows.

Suppose that there is data on K inputs and M outputs on each of N firms, or DMUs as they are referred to in the DEA literature. For the $i^{th}$ DMU these are represented by the vectors $x_i$ and $y_i$, respectively. The KxN input matrix, X, and the MxN output matrix, Y, represent the data of all the DMUs. DEA constructs a non-parametric envelopment frontier over the data points such that all observed points lie on or below the production frontier.

DEA is best introduced by means of ratio form. For each DMU (specifically a primary school in the case of this article) one seeks to obtain a measure of the ratio of all outputs over all inputs, which takes the following form, $\frac{u'y_i}{v'x_i}$, where $u$ is an Mx1 vector of output weights and $v$ is a Kx1 vector of input weights. In order to select optimal weights, the following mathematical programming problem is specified:

$$\begin{aligned} &Max_{u,v}\left[\frac{u'y_i}{v'x_i}\right] \\ &subject \quad to \\ &\frac{u'y_j}{v'x_j} \leq 1, \quad j = 1,2,....,N \\ &u, v \geq 0 \end{aligned} \tag{1}$$

The mathematical programming problem entails finding values for $u$ and $v$, such that the efficiency measure of the $i^{th}$ primary school is maximised subject to the constraint that the overall efficiency measures must be equal to or less than unity (one). However the ratio formulation has a disadvantage of having an infinite number of solutions. For instance, if $(u^*, v^*)$ is a solution, then $(\alpha u^*, \alpha v^*)$ is another possible solution, amongst others. To address this problem one can impose the constraint $v'x_i = 1$, which yields equation (2):

$$\begin{aligned} &Max_{\mu,v}[\mu' y_i] \\ &subject \quad to \\ &v'x_i = 1, \\ &\mu' y_j - v'x_j \leq 0, \quad j = 1,2,...,N, \\ &\mu, v \geq 0, \end{aligned} \tag{2}$$

where the notation change from $u$ and ' to $\mu$ and $\nu$ reflects the transformation. This form is known as the *multiplier* form of the linear programming problem.

By means of duality in linear programming, one can derive an equivalent envelopment form of this problem (Coelli, 1996):

$$
\begin{aligned}
& Min_{\theta,\lambda}\theta \\
& subject \quad to \\
& -y_i + Y\lambda \geq 0, \\
& \theta x_i - X\lambda \geq 0, \\
& \lambda \geq 0
\end{aligned}
\tag{3}
$$

where $\theta$ is a scalar and $\lambda$ is an Nx1 vector of constants. This envelopment form entails fewer constraints than the multiplier form (K+M □ N+1) and therefore is the generally preferable form to solve. The value of $\theta$ obtained is the efficiency score for the $i^{th}$ school. It has to satisfy $0 \leq \theta \leq 1$, with a value of 1 showing a point on the production frontier. It is therefore a technically efficient school according to Farrell's (1957) definition. It is worth noting that the linear programming problem must be solved N times, once for each school in the sample to yield a value of $\theta$.

The CRS assumption is only appropriate when all schools operate at an optimal scale. Constraints in the operating environment may cause a school to operate at non-optimal scale. Banker et al (1984) suggest an extension of the CRS DEA model to provide for Variable Returns to Scale (VRS) situations. The use of the CRS specification when not all schools are operating at the optimal scale results in a measure of technical efficiency that is confounded by scale efficiency. The use of the VRS DEA specification permits the calculation of scale inefficiency.

The CRS linear programming problem can be modified to account for VRS by adding the convexity constraint $N1'\lambda = 1$ to equation (3), where N1 is an Nx1 vector of ones (Coelli, 1996). This approach forms a convex hull of intersecting planes, which envelop the data points more tightly than the CRS canonical hull and thus provide technical efficiency scores which are equal to or greater than those obtainable by the CRS model.

## 4. Unit of Analysis, Data Type, Sources, and Sample Size

This study investigated the technical efficiency and total factor productivity growth of Uganda's primary schools. The study's unit of analysis is a primary school. A stratified random sample of 500 primary schools (200 public, 150 private, and 150 community-owned) in Uganda over the 1995-2009 period was selected. Input data to various primary schools were obtained from the planning department of the Ministry of Education and Sports. Educational output data relating to the academic achievement by students were obtained from the Uganda National Examinations Board.

Education is a transforming process in which policies, practices, and environmental qualities, operating at the student, classroom, school, and district levels, impact teaching and learning. Resources or inputs, such as school buildings, teachers, books, and technology, help develop each student's potential. At the same time, students bring inputs of their own, including abilities, attitudes, and the influences and resources of families and communities. In what follows, we discuss how we constructed input and output variables.

### Output Variables

True educational output is very difficult to measure empirically due to its inherent intangibility. Education does not only consist of the ability to repeat information and answer questions, but it also involves the skills to interpret information and learn how to behave in society. In spite of the multi-product nature of education, most studies have used the results obtained in cognitive tests since they are difficult to manipulate and respond to administration demands. Hoxby (2000) notes that the most important reason for using these results could be that both policymakers and parents use this criterion to choose schools for their children.

The study's output measures focus on the process type or production volume style estimates of educational output. The study examined four measures of primary schools' output in the Primary Leaving Examinations (PLE): division 1, division 2, division 3, and division 4. Student academic achievement, as measured by examinations and other test scores, has been the most extensively studied educational benefit both in the developed and developing worlds (Simmons & Alexander, 1978). A school embraces various resources in a series of processes that ultimately aim to improve upon the educational achievement of students and contribute to literate communities. Below are the details with regard to the educational output variables constructed.

- Division 1 comprises the number of pupils who passed PLE with division 1. Qualifying for division 1 entails getting between 4 and 12 aggregates.
- Division 2 comprises the number of pupils who passed PLE with division 2. Qualifying for division 2 entails getting between 13 and 23 aggregates.
- Division 3 comprises the number of pupils who passed PLE with division 3. Qualifying for division 3 entails getting between 24 and 29 aggregates.
- Division 4 comprises the number of pupils who passed PLE with division 4. Qualifying for division 4 entails getting between 30 and 34 aggregates.

## Input Variables

Sutherland et al (2009) note that two sets of inputs determine educational outcomes, namely discretionary and nondiscretionary. Discretionary inputs include factors under the control of the education system and can be defined in physical inputs, such as number of teachers, teacher-student ratios, class sizes, instruction time, teacher quality, and, to a lesser extent, other resources in schools. The non-discretionary inputs cover environmental inputs, which are not amenable to direct control. Student achievement is considered to be dependent upon, amongst other factors, family and peer-group effects and innate ability. While difficult to measure, these factors are often proxied by measures of socio-economic status.

Five inputs are constructed, namely teachers, pupils, classrooms, toilets, and average class size. The input of teachers includes the total number of teachers in each primary school irrespective of level of education. The numbers of toilet cubicles are lumped together and are not decomposed by sex. Jaiyeoba and Atanda (2011) note that toilets (conveniences) represent one of the strong school-based quality factors that contributes to students' academic achievement. Average class size is constructed by dividing the total student population by the number of classrooms in a primary school. This variable is usually considered a school input in efficiency analysis, according to the results of some studies in which a direct relationship is found between reduced class size and higher academic performance (Card & Krueger, 1992; Hoxby, 2000; Krueger, 2003; Mora et al, 2010). Other studies conclude that this variable is not significant (Hanushek, 2003; Pritchett & Filmer, 1999).

**Table 1 Definition and Measurement of Input and Output Variables**

| *Variables* | *Definition* |
|---|---|
| *Outputs* | |
| Division 1 | Number of pupils who passed Primary Leaving Examinations with division one (i.e. 4-12 aggregates). |
| Division 2 | Number of pupils who passed Primary Leaving Examinations with division two (i.e. 13-23 aggregates). |
| Division 3 | Number of pupils who passed Primary Leaving Examinations with division three (i.e. 24-29 aggregates). |
| Division 4 | Number of pupils who passed Primary Leaving Examinations with division four (i.e. 30-34 aggregates). |
| *Inputs* | |
| Teachers | Total number of teachers in a given primary school. |
| Pupils | The total number of pupils in a primary school. |
| Classrooms | Total number of classrooms in a primary school. |
| Toilets | Total number of toilets in the school. |
| Average class size | Total student population divided by the number of classrooms. |

Table 1 presents the article's definition and measurement of the input and output variables. In nonparametric data envelopment analysis when we deal with multi-inputs and multi-outputs, we do not have straightforward hypotheses. All we can hypothesise is that decision-making units with an efficiency score of 1 or 100% are deemed technically efficient, while those whose scores are less than 1 or 100% are inefficient. It is the case that when super-efficiency is analysed, efficiency scores can exceed 100%.

## 5. Empirical Results

The empirical results are discussed under the following headings: descriptive statistical analysis, correlation analysis, and technical efficiency.

### Descriptive Statistical Analysis

The descriptive statistics of the educational inputs and outputs for 500 schools over the 1995-2009 period are presented in Table 2. The table indicates that the mean number of teachers in the sampled primary schools stood at about 12 teachers with a standard deviation of 6 teachers. Considering that a primary school has seven classes with several streams, the average number of teachers in Uganda's primary schools is far below the number necessary to adequately attend to the learners to produce satisfactory academic achievement. Turning to the number of pupils in the sampled schools, it emerges that the average number of pupils in the sampled schools stood at 711 with a standard deviation of 344. The average number of classrooms in the sampled schools stood at 17 with a standard deviation of about 10. This in turn, translates into an average class size of 70 pupils (this is higher than the recommended class size of 40) with a standard deviation of 160. It is clear that classes in Uganda's primary schools are overcrowded. USAID (2007) notes that overcrowded or large classrooms are those where the pupil-teacher ratios exceed 40:1. Primary teachers in Uganda face many obstacles when attempting to teach in overcrowded classes.

Turning to the average educational outputs, the average number of pupils who attained division 1 stood at 2 with a standard deviation of 10. The mean number of pupils who attained division 2 stood at 14 with a standard deviation of approximately 15. The mean number of pupils who attained division 3 stood at 12 with a standard deviation of about 9 pupils; while the mean number of students who attained division 4 stood at about 8 with a standard deviation of about 6 pupils.

**Table 2 Mean and Standard Deviation of Input and Output Variables, Pooled Dataset 1995-2009**

| Variable | Mean | Standard Deviation | Sample Variance | Kurtosis | Skewness | Range |
|---|---|---|---|---|---|---|
| Division 1 | 2.16 | 10.19 | 103.93 | 290.87 | 15.85 | 199.00 |
| Division 2 | 14.22 | 14.77 | 218.23 | 24.35 | 3.72 | 143.00 |
| Division 3 | 12.47 | 8.57 | 73.37 | 13.71 | 2.18 | 91.00 |
| Division 4 | 7.97 | 5.58 | 31.18 | 1.80 | 1.21 | 33.00 |
| Teachers | 11.70 | 5.75 | 33.09 | 1.36 | 0.98 | 31.00 |
| Pupils | 711.51 | 344.38 | 118597.48 | 1.49 | 0.96 | 2253.00 |
| Toilets | 13.18 | 9.97 | 99.39 | 4.94 | 1.65 | 70.00 |
| Classrooms | 17.52 | 9.81 | 96.29 | 1.79 | 0.84 | 66.00 |
| Average Class Size | 70.37 | 160.71 | 25826.56 | 79.70 | 8.26 | 2026.68 |

## Correlation Analysis

Table 3 presents the Pearson correlation matrix of input and output variables for the pooled dataset (1995-2009) with a total of 7,500 observations. Some correlation coefficients are significant while others are not. We report both the significant and insignificant correlation coefficients, especially those with implications on the resources at the disposal of the sampled schools.

It is clear from Table 3 that divisions 3 and 4 are highly and positively correlated. This implies that a primary school, which had many of its pupils in either division, had a high likelihood of having more pupils in the other. The number of teachers was highly and positively correlated with the number of pupils. The number of classrooms and toilets was positively and highly correlated. Average class size was negatively correlated with divisions 2, 3, and 4. This therefore implies that overcrowded classes are likely to work against the academic performance of students.

The principal technical efficiency results reported in this section were derived by allowing for variable returns to scale. Variable returns to scale results are presented because they are more plausible in the real-world, where decision-making units operate in less than optimal conditions. The mean technical efficiency scores differed by location and ownership. Table 4 presents the mean constant returns to scale, variable returns to scale, and scale efficiency scores by region, as well as ownership and rural-urban divides.

**Table 3 Pearson Correlation Matrix of Input and Output Variables, Pooled Dataset 1995-2009**

| | (1) | (2) | (3) | (4) | (5) | (6) | (7) | (8) | (9) |
|---|---|---|---|---|---|---|---|---|---|
| (1) Division 1 | 1.00 | | | | | | | | |
| (2) Division 2 | 0.29 | 1.00 | | | | | | | |
| (3) Division 3 | 0.02 | 0.38 | 1.00 | | | | | | |
| (4) Division 4 | -0.09 | 0.08 | 0.61 | 1.00 | | | | | |
| (5) Total-teachers | -0.01 | -0.02 | 0.01 | 0.02 | 1.00 | | | | |
| (6) Total Pupils | 0.02 | -0.04 | -0.01 | 0.02 | 0.76 | 1.00 | | | |
| (7) Toilets | 0.02 | 0.02 | 0.02 | 0.03 | 0.51 | 0.47 | 1.00 | | |
| (8) Classrooms | 0.01 | -0.01 | 0.04 | 0.06 | 0.64 | 0.55 | 0.56 | 1.00 | |
| (9) Average Class Size | 0.01 | -0.01 | -0.03 | -0.02 | 0.07 | 0.08 | -0.14 | -0.38 | 1.00 |

**Table 4 Mean Technical Efficiency Scores (Constant Returns to Scale, Variable Returns to Scale, and Scale Efficiency), 1995-2009**

| | Constant Returns to Scale Technical Efficiency (CRS TE) | Variable Returns to Scale Technical Efficiency (VRS TE) | Scale Efficiency $= \frac{CRS \quad TE}{VRS \quad TE}$ |
|---|---|---|---|
| National | 0.856 | 0.944 | 0.905 |
| *Urban* | 0.844 | 0.943 | 0.895 |
| *Rural* | 0.719 | 0.779 | 0.923 |
| Regions | | | |
| *Central* | 0.975 | 0.985 | 0.989 |
| *Eastern* | 0.791 | 0.864 | 0.916 |
| *Northern* | 0.765 | 0.897 | 0.853 |
| *Western* | 0.911 | 0.912 | 0.998 |
| Ownership | | | |
| *Public* | 0.805 | 0.859 | 0.938 |
| *Private* | 0.949 | 0.973 | 0.975 |
| *Community* | 0.535 | 0.943 | 0.567 |

At the national level, the constant returns to scale technical efficiency score stands at 0.856, while the variable returns to scale technical efficiency score stands at 0.944, which yields a scale efficiency score of 0.905. Along the rural-urban divide, urban primary schools are more technically efficient (with a VRS technical efficiency score of 0.943) compared to rural schools (0.779). At the regional level, the Central Region is technically more efficient, with a VRS technical efficiency score of 0.985, followed by the Western (0.912), Northern (0.897), and Eastern (0.864) Regions. By ownership, privately owned schools are more technically efficient (0.973), followed by community-owned schools/faith-based schools (0.943) and public schools (0.859). Technical efficiency scores only refer to the relative performance within the sample. Primary schools with an efficiency score of one are efficient relative to all other schools in the sample, but may not be efficient by some absolute standard. Inefficiency is inherently unobservable – all we can do is benchmark primary schools against each other, not against some absolute standard.

In what follows, the technical efficiency results are linked to discretionary variables. To accomplish this, schools were arbitrarily categorised into three cohorts: low performers (with a mean VRS technical efficiency score in the 53 – 70% bracket); moderate performers (with a mean VRS technical efficiency score in the 71 – 85% range); and high performers (with a mean VRS technical efficiency score in the 86 – 100% range). Table 5 presents the means of the discretionary variables for the three categories.

**Table 5 Means of Discretionary Variables by Category of Performance, 1995-2009**

| Discretionary Variable | Low Performers (VRS TE: 53-70%) | Moderate Performers (VRS TE: 71-85%) | High Performers (VRS TE: 85-100%) |
|---|---|---|---|
| Teachers | 8.8 | 23.4 | 52.7 |
| Pupils | 1067.3 | 925.0 | 853.8 |
| Classrooms | 9.9 | 26.4 | 39.5 |
| Toilets | 13.1 | 35.0 | 52.6 |
| Average Class Size | 140.7 | 105.6 | 52.8 |

As indicated in Table 5, there is a direct relationship between the numbers of teachers, classrooms, and toilets and a school's technical efficiency score. Conversely, there is an inverse relationship between technical efficiency and the number of pupils and average class size. This implies that big classes adversely affect academic achievement.

This study also attempted to link the technical efficiency scores of the various cohorts of schools to the following non-discretionary variables: regional poverty levels, regional parental literacy, teacher effort, and teacher remuneration. There are marked differences between rural and urban poverty levels in Uganda, with poverty remaining higher in rural areas than in urban areas. Rural areas account for 85% of the population but 94.4% of the poor, while urban areas account for 15% of the population but only 5.6% of the poor. As of the fiscal year 2009/10, the proportion of the total population that is poor by region was as follows: 2.7% in Central Region; 6.9% in Eastern Region; 8.9% in Northern Region; and 5% in Western Region (Republic of Uganda, 2011).

There is a correlation between regional poverty levels and a given region's mean technical efficiency score of its primary schools. The Central Region, with the lowest proportion of poor people (2.7%), has the highest technical efficiency score (0.975), followed by the Western Region (0.911). There is an inverse relationship between educational achievement and poverty levels across regions. Similar results have been found by other researchers. For instance, Lacour and Tissington (2011) investigated the effects of poverty on academic achievement in the United States. They found that low achievement is closely correlated with lack of resources.

Parental involvement is associated with higher student achievement outcomes. However, parental involvement is also determined by the literacy of parents. In Uganda, according to the 2009/10 household survey results, the percentage of households that had never attended school stood at 13.9% in Northern Region; 8% in Central Region; 11.4% in Western Region; and 7.9% in Eastern Region (Republic of Uganda, 2011). By approximately linking a region's literacy level to its academic achievement, it emerges that the Central Region, with 8% of people who have never attended school (or a literary rate of 92%), has the highest technical efficiency of primary schools (97.5%). On the other hand, the Northern Region, with the lowest literacy rate of 86%, has the lowest level of technical efficiency (76.5%).

Teacher effort is an important input into learning. The most crucial forms of quiet corruption in education are teacher absence and low effort while in school. Evidence on the extent of teacher absence has improved greatly over the last decade. Early evidence comes from head-teacher or teacher self-reports of the duration of absence during a given time period (usually 1 – 4 weeks). According to a World Bank study, more than half the teachers in Tanzania and Uganda were absent at least one day in the previous week, and about a quarter of teachers were absent for two or more days. In Uganda, head teachers were twice as likely to be absent as regular teachers. Nearly one-third of teachers were not in the classroom during learning periods (World Bank, 2010).

Schools combine instructional materials and teacher and pupil interaction to produce cognitive skills. The World Bank (2010) documents the leakage of two key inputs, namely instructional materials and school inspection. A teacher with few or no instructional materials will find it harder to impart the necessary skills to his or her charges. Additionally, school inspection ensures that the right pedagogical strategies are being implemented and instructional materials are well deployed. The clearest example of the extent of leakage of instructional resources comes from two PETS surveys in Uganda in the 1990s. The first study revealed that an average of only 13% of the resources intended for schools were reaching them. In addition, more than 70% of students were in schools that had not been inspected in the previous year.

Teacher motivation and incentives in order to increase student performance is an increasingly popular education policy around the world. Fryer (2011) describes a school-based randomised trial in over 200 New York City public schools designed to better understand the impact of teacher incentives on student achievement. No evidence is found that teacher incentives increase student performance, attendance, or graduation, nor is there any evidence that the incentives change student or teacher behaviour. It should be noted that, currently, a primary school teacher in Uganda earns Sh.260,000 (approximately US$100) per month, while secondary schools teachers receive about Sh.450,000 (Mubiru, 2010). These figures are out of touch with the rising costs of living. The poor academic achievement can to some extent be blamed on poor teacher remuneration and unfavourable working conditions.

## 6. Discussion and Further Research

The technical efficiency of some primary schools in the sample is less than 100%. This should be of some concern to policy makers and planners interested in good value for money. Given the existing levels of both technical and scale inefficiency, the attainment of the national education objectives, as well as education-related global and regional targets such as the Dakar Framework for Action and the Millennium Development Goals, will be compromised. The efficient use of existing resources should be the centrepiece of the country's education policy.

Nevertheless, the degree of inefficiency is high, and the policy response should be contingent upon the primary school's operating environment. Appropriate action ought to be taken only after a thorough investigation. DEA is an important indicator that may serve as the point of departure for decisions on funding or resource distribution. Naturally, these kinds of decisions must also consider the specific circumstances (beyond the control of the schools) that individual schools have to face in terms of socio-economic differences, where, for example, operating in a 'disadvantaged area' would mean that a specific school needs more resources.

Technical and scale inefficiency are present in varying degrees in a majority of schools in both developing and developed countries. For instance, Mizala et al (2002) assessed the technical efficiency of Chilean schools. According to their DEA results, a typical school has an efficiency of 95%, while the range is from 53% to 100%. Hu et al (2009) report that half of the schools sampled from Beijing primary schools reach technical and scale efficiency, with an average technical value of 0.90, which is an optimistic result, although some of the schools were low in technical efficiency. Academic performance has also been found to be dictated by the functionality of facilities. For example, USAID (2009) notes that higher performing schools in Ghana are more likely to have electricity and functional toilets. High performing schools also tended to be located in urban areas.

This article estimated the technical efficiency and total factor productivity growth of Uganda's primary schools. As a follow-up to this study, there are myriad areas that merit further investigation. There is a dearth of knowledge with regard to the extent to which Uganda's primary schools are provided with discretionary and non-discretionary resources in fulfilling their mandates. Academic achievement is also affected by student characteristics (parental and community involvement) and other environmental factors. It would be intuitive to find out how student attributes interact with the school characteristics as well as the community variables to impact upon academic achievement. Parent involvement has been shown to be an important variable that positively influences children's education. More schools have observed its importance and are encouraging families to become more involved. Because of this trend, it is essential to understand what is meant by parental involvement and in what ways it influences children's education.

Given that this article has demonstrated that private schools are relatively more technically efficient than public and community schools, there is need to find out what accounts for this state of affairs. We do not know the internal efficiency of primary education in Uganda and the drivers of regional differences in technical efficiency. There is need to find out the lessons that public and community schools can draw from private schools to enhance their performance in the spirit of public-private partnerships for education.

## 7. Conclusion

The following conclusions emerge from this study. The mean technical efficiency scores differ by location and ownership. The technical efficiency results are affected by discretionary and non-discretionary variables. There is a direct relationship between the numbers of teachers, classrooms, and toilets and a school's technical efficiency score. Conversely, there is an inverse relationship between technical efficiency and the number of pupils, as well as the average class size. This implies that big classes adversely affect academic achievement. There is a correlation between regional poverty levels and a given region's mean technical efficiency score of its primary schools. There is an inverse relationship between educational achievement and poverty levels across regions.

Parental involvement is associated with higher student achievement outcomes. However, parental involvement is also determined by the literacy of parents. If schools operate under low efficiency, the resources will not be properly utilised and the sustainability of education will not be ensured. One of the most important challenges to Uganda's primary education sub-sector is low technical efficiency.

Educational quality is the key object of schools. The indicators of teachers' salaries, student-teacher ratios, and the time students spend in school have an obvious effect on schools' technical efficiency. Considering the status-quo of Uganda's primary schools, we suggest that teachers' salaries be increased. Additionally, there is need to reduce student-teacher ratios, provide better toilet facilities, and address teacher absenteeism, which impacts on the quality of time that students spend at school. These initiatives will help schools scale-up their technical efficiency.

## 8. Policy Implications

The article has various policy implications. The technical efficiency results were linked to discretionary and non-discretionary variables. There is a direct relationship between the numbers of teachers, classrooms, and toilets and a school's technical efficiency score. Conversely, there is an inverse relationship between technical efficiency and the number of pupils as well as average class size. This result implies that big classes adversely affect academic achievement. The study also attempted to link the technical efficiency scores of the various cohorts of schools to some non-discretionary variables. There is a correlation between regional poverty levels and a given region's mean technical efficiency score of its primary schools. The Central Region, with the lowest proportion of poor people (2.7%), has the highest technical efficiency score (0.975), followed by the Western Region (0.911). There is an inverse relationship between educational achievement and poverty levels across regions.

Parental involvement is associated with higher student achievement outcomes. However, parental involvement is also determined by the literacy of parents. Linking a region's literacy level to its academic achievement shows that the Central Region, with the highest literary rate of 92%, has the highest technical efficiency of primary schools (97.5%). On the other hand, the Northern Region, with the lowest literacy rate of 86%, has the lowest level of technical efficiency (76.5%).

This study demonstrated that Uganda's primary schools are technically inefficient. Given that there is clearly a resource gap in terms of physical and human infrastructure (classrooms, toilets, and teachers), one can be tempted to conjecture that they are doing their best within the limitations posed by the available resources. There are schools in both rural and urban areas that are under-resourced, with ratios of over 100 pupils per teacher.

It has been found that higher pupil-teacher ratios adversely affect academic achievement and thereby the technical efficiency of schools. The pupil-classroom ratios (average class size) are far higher than the corresponding pupil-teacher ratios. This suggests that there are many classes that take place in non-classroom environments, which inconveniences pupils and teachers due to class-transfers, especially when the weather conditions change. There is an urgent need to increase the number of classrooms, number of teachers, and toilet facilities.

## Notes

[1] The author acknowledges the invaluable comments by resource persons and participants at the biannual workshops of 2009 and 2010 organised by the African Economic Research Consortium (AERC). The AERC is further appreciated for the research grant that facilitated my undertaking this study.

## References

Ajibefun, I. A. 2008. 'An Evaluation of Parametric and Non-Parametric Methods of Technical Efficiency Measurement: Application to Small Scale Food Crop Production in Nigeria'. *Journal of Agriculture and Social Sciences* 4: 95-100.

Banker, R. D., A. Charnes, and W. W. Cooper. 1984. 'Models for Estimating Technical and Scale Efficiencies in Data Envelopment Analysis'. *Management Science* 30, no. 9: 1078-92.

Card, D. and A. Krueger. 1992. 'Does School Quality Matter? Returns to Education and the Characteristics of Public Schools in the United States'. *Journal of Political Economy* 100: 1-40.

Charnes, A., W. W. Cooper, E. and Rhodes. 1978. 'Measuring the Efficiency of Decision Making Units'. *European Journal of Operational Research* 2: 429-44.

Coelli, T. J. 1996. 'A Guide to DEAP Version 2.1: A Data Envelopment Analysis (Computer) Program'. Centre for Efficiency and Productivity Analysis (CEPA) Working Paper 96/8. Department of Econometrics, University of New England, Australia.

Fryer, R. G. 2011. 'Teacher Incentives and Student Achievement: Evidence from New York City Public Schools'. National Bureau of Economic Research, NBER Working Paper Series, Working Paper 16850.

Hanushek, E. A. 2003. 'The Failure of Input Based Schooling Policies'. *The Economic Journal* 113: 64-98.

Hoxby, C. M. 2000. 'The Effects of Class Size on Student Achievement: New Evidence from Population Variation'. *Quarterly Journal of Economics* 115: 1239-85.

Hu, Y., Z. Zhang, and W.Liang. 2009. 'Efficiency of Primary Schools in Beijing, China: An Evaluation by Data Envelopment Analysis'. *International Journal of Educational Management* 23, no. 1: 34-50.

Jaiyeoba, A. O. and A. I. Atanda. 2011. 'School Quality Factors and Secondary School Students' Achievement in Mathematics in South-Western and North-Central Nigeria'. *The African Symposium* 11, no. 1: 91-100.

Krueger, A. B. 2003. 'Economic Considerations and Class Size'. *Economic Journal* 113: 34-63.

Lacour, M. and L. D. Tissington. 2011. 'The Effects of Poverty on Academic Achievement'. *Educational Research and Reviews* 6, no. 7: 522-27.

Ministry of Education and Sports. 2000. 'Teacher Utilization Studies; Volume I: A Draft Report on Primary Schools'. Kampala: Ministry of Education and Sports.

Mizala, A., P. Romaguera, and D. Farren. 2002. 'The Technical Efficiency of Schools in Chile'. *Applied Econometrics* 34: 1533-52.

Mora, T., J. O. Escardibul, and M. Espasa. 2010. 'The Effects of Regional Educational Policies on School Failure in Spain'. *Revista de Economía Aplicada*: 1-28.

Mubiru, A. 2010. 'Teachers Call off Strike, to Meet Museveni'. *The New Vision*. 26 July 2010: 13.

Nishimura, M., K. Ogawa, D. N. Sifuna, J. Chimombo, D. Kunje, J. G. Ampiah, A. Byamugisha, N. Sawamura, and S. Yamada. 2009. 'A Comparative Analysis of Universal Primary Education Policy in Ghana, Kenya, Malawi, and Uganda'. *Journal of International Cooperation in Education* 12, no. 1: 143-58.

Pritchett, L. and D. Filmer. 1999. 'What Education Production Functions Really Show: A Positive Theory of Education Expenditures'. *Economics of Education Review* 18: 223-39.

Republic of Uganda. 2010. *Budget Speech, Financial Year 2010/11*. Kampala: Ministry of Finance, Planning and Economic Development.

—. 2011. *The Background to the Budget 2011/12 Fiscal Year*. Kampala: Ministry of Finance, Planning and Economic Development.

Simmons, J., and L. Alexander. 1978. 'The Determinants of School Achievement in Developing Countries: A Review of the Research'. *Economic Development and Cultural Change* 26: 341-57.

Sutherland, D., R. Price, and F. Gonnand. 2009. 'Improving Public Spending Efficiency in Primary and Secondary Education'. *OECD Journal: Economic* Studies: 1-30.

Todd, P. E. and K. Wolpin. 2003. 'On the Specification and Estimation of the Production Function for Cognitive Achievement'. *Economic Journal* 113: F3-F33.

Transparency International. 2010. *Africa Education Watch: Good Governance Lessons for Primary Education.*

Uganda Bureau of Statistics. 2010. *2010 Statistical* Abstract. Kampala: Uganda Bureau of Statistics.

UNESCO. 2004. *Public Expenditure Tracking Surveys in Education.* Paris: International Institute for Educational Planning.

USAID. 2007. 'Large Class Sizes in the Developing World: What Do We Know and What Can We Do?' http://pdf.usaid.gov/pdf_docs/PNADK328.pdf (accessed 5 May 2011).

—. 2009. 'Review of Basic Education Quality in Ghana; Basic Education in Ghana: Progress and Problems'. http://ddp-ext.worldbank.org/EdStats/GHAdprep09.pdf (accessed 6 May 2011).

World Bank. 2010. *Silent and Lethal: How Quiet Corruption Undermines Africa's Development Efforts*. Washington, DC: The World Bank.

# FEASIBILITY OF TAXING THE INFORMAL SECTOR: A SURVEY WITH REFLECTIONS ON TANZANIA

LONGINUS RUTASITARA

*This article discusses the feasibility of mobilising tax revenue from the informal sector in a developing country context, where the informal sector is growing but is largely going untaxed. The expansion of the tax base may be enhanced by supporting the productive capacities of informal sector activities through innovative formalisation interventions that seek to break the growth-constraints faced by more enterprising informal sector operators. While the impact of tax rates and tax administration on the informal sector is better understood (shared with formal small and medium enterprises, to some extent), more research is needed about the determinants of tax non-compliance of the sector. Because of the heterogeneity of the informal sector, it is proposed that studying the impact of formalisation interventions and tax compliance behaviour selection may be made up of specific activities (informal sector sub-sectors). This will lead to the better management of research, as well as the design and implementation of tax regimes for the informal sector.*

## 1. Introduction

Like in many developing countries, interest in the economic significance of the informal sector in Tanzania is growing, particularly with regard to the sector's contribution to growth and tax revenue. At least two observations support the need to tap the tax potential of the informal sector. First, the informal sector takes up a significant, and others reckon, a rising, share of GDP – from 20% to 60% (IFC, 2007; Schneider, 2002; Stern & Barbour, 2005). Second, developing countries' tax bases are narrow as they rely on a few tax payers for government revenue (Gërxhani, 2004; Glenday, 2007). Large tax payers, who make up less than 1% of the registered payers, contribute 70% or more of the tax revenue; whereas small and medium tax payers (70% plus of the total tax payers) contribute from 0% to 25% of the total tax revenue (IFC, 2007). Growing public spending needs and budget deficits imply that revenue from the formal sector and foreign aid are not adequate; this makes the informal sector a compelling option for expanding domestic revenue (Fosu & Drine, 2009; Glenday, 2007).

An expanding non-tax paying informal economy undermines domestic revenue mobilisation and equity. Overtaxing a shrinking formal sector distorts the natural competitive process by giving an unfair cost advantage to the informal sector operators (Lewis, 2004). It leads to lower compliance morale among compliant formal tax payers, a rise in tax avoidance, and a fall in tax revenue. Thus, to broaden the tax base and enhance equity, it is necessary to bring the informal sector into the tax net (UNECA, 2009; Moyi & Ronge, 2006).

Two views feature in the discussion of the taxable capacity of the informal sector in developing country conditions. The first view would suggest that there is low direct revenue potential from the informal sector. This is because informal sector activities are characteristically limited by their small scale of operation and hence low levels of profits. The second view, however, sees the possibility of growth of the informal activities if necessary institutional support is availed to them to both foster their productive capacity (growth) and therefore their ability to pay taxes, with some level of compliance to regulations (Ayee, 2007; Di John, 2008; Bird, 2008). However, the ease with which informal sector operators can hide away from the tax net and other regulations makes collection of taxes from the informal sector on a sustainable basis quite daunting.

Based on a survey of literature, this article discusses the feasibility of taxing the informal sector in developing countries and makes reflections on the Tanzanian situation. What should governments know and do better in order to tap the tax potential of the informal sector? In agreement with most analysts, it is proposed that the strategy to raise domestic revenue should target improvement of the productive capacities of selected informal sector operators. Long-term tax revenue is possible once their growth-constraints are eased. Also, an understanding of the informal sector operators' tax compliance behaviour is necessary.

Section II reviews the main concepts and describes experiences in other countries regarding taxing the informal sector. Sector III brings in insights on policy interventions and the experience of Tanzania. Section

IV raises follow-up questions and possible research issues. Section V makes concluding remarks.

## 2. Conceptual Framework and Literature Review

### The Informal Sector Defined

The term informal is described in many different ways. In economics, it is commonly used to refer to output and labour that are not registered with government or registered firm or unreported activities (Palmade & Anayiotos, 2005). The informal activities and informal employment are not recorded on official statistics, avoid government regulations, and do not pay taxes (Gërxhani, 2004). Though such activities were taking place long before the 1970s, the concept was coined in 1972 by the International Labour Organisation (ILO) in its Kenya Mission Report, which characterised the informal sector as easy to enter in (and exit from), relying on indigenous resources, owned by family, and small in scale of operations. It was labour intensive, using low technology and operating in unregulated and competitive markets (ILO, 1972).

In subsequent years, the concept was integrated into different international and national programmes with a view largely to easing the growth-constraints of the sector. According to Bangansser (2000), the 1980s were mainly dispersion years, when the concept spread amongst various technical departments of government and development agencies. The 1990s are known as the ‘officialisation’ years, notably 1993, in which the 15th International Conference of Labour Statisticians (ICLS) for standards on informal sector statistics and revision of the international System of National Accounts (SNA) incorporated the informal sector (ibid., p. 2). The 2000s onwards are formalisation years, aimed at further integrating the informal sector into the formal economy. Though emphasis is on elevating the growth prospects of the informal sector, including ‘decent jobs’ in all places of work, keen emphasis is placed on mobilising tax revenue from this sector (Chen, 2007; Engelschalk & Loeprick, 2007; Palmade & Anayiotos, 2005).

The present discussion focuses on the productive and service-oriented informal activities or product informality (it leaves out labour informality). The productive activities in question are undertaken by ‘poor’ or ‘low-income’ households or firms as a way of coping with stress (pursuing survival) and hoping to grow once the critical constraints of capital, technology, and markets are relaxed. The activities range from service provision (e.g. street vending, pavement food stalls), craftsmanship (such as mechanics, masons, and carpenters), and other light manufacturing activities. Their services or products cater for the low income populations in the neighbourhood (Bigsten, Kimunyu, & Lundvall, 2004; Araujo-Bonjean & Chambas, 2003), and there is a symbiotic linkage between the formal and informal sectors, in for instance, the sale of products and sourcing of inputs.

The informal activities in question are legal, and the commodities are not harmful to consumers or society at large, except to the extent that they avoid regulations and do not pay taxes and essentially free-ride on public utilities such as roads, street lighting, etc. The discussion does not deal with informal illicit activities and products. Araujo-Bonjean and Chambas (2003) and Tripp (1996), among others, identify such activities with the abuse of formal institutions for fraudulent purposes - drug trafficking, money-laundering, sex work where it is not legalised, smuggling, insider-trading, moonlighting etc. These activities often fetch huge profits that are not declared or taxed. Such tax-evading activities are run by operators who are by no means low-income. The activities can be sophisticated, hard-to-detect, and harmful to society. The goal of policy then is to curb these activities, and not to mobilise government revenue from them.

## Rise of Informality in the Developing Countries

In the 1950s and 1960s, economies of developing countries were described as dualistic in nature, with a potentially expanding modern capitalist sector and a traditional rural subsistence sector that had an excess supply of largely unskilled labour. The growing 'industrial wage sector' would gradually absorb the low productivity 'traditional non-wage sector' through rural-to-urban migration (Harris & Todaro, 1970). As the new arrivals from rural areas exceeded what the industrial sector could absorb, the urban economy began exhibiting dual features – the formal and informal sectors. The urban formal sector depicted a modernising industrial sector, while the informal sector comprised arrivals from the rural areas, who, having failed to secure a wage paying job, resorted to either creating their own employment or working for small-scale family-owned enterprises (Swaminathan, 1991). Although the wages in the formal sector were kept low due to the existence of surplus labour migrating from rural areas, the average urban formal sector incomes remained higher than those in the (urban) informal sector. But urban informal-sector average incomes remained persistently higher than rural average incomes. In large part this explains the continued rural-to-urban migration and an expanding urban informal sector (Todaro & Smith, 2009).

A further dimension of informality has been located in the rural areas in the form of rural-non-farm activities (RNFAs) (Davis, 2003; Barret, Reardon, & Webb, 2001; Gordon & Craig, 2001; Islam, 1997). Many of the RNFAs apparently offer higher average incomes compared to subsistence agriculture. Most of the RNFAs are not regulated or taxed. Rural investment climate surveys have identified characteristics and constraints facing the RNFAs that are similar to urban informal and formal small and medium scale enterprises (SMEs) (World Bank, 2006; World Bank, 2008). Determining how the average incomes of RNFAs compare with urban informal sector incomes and the influence of the growth of RNFAs on rural-to-urban migration are empirical matters.

The informal sector, which was earlier viewed as destined to be replaced by a formal, modern sector with regular paid jobs, has thus continued to grow and become more complex, and it is seen as playing a potential developmental role, not simply acting as a mere safety-net or survival strategy (Chen, 2007). This view boldly implies that the informal sector can be dynamic and achieve high levels of productivity through formalisation incentives. It is posited that in many African countries, the informal sector is increasingly accommodating even the better educated and skilled labour force who are forced to venture into self-employment to supplement their incomes (Theis, 2005; Sookram & Watson, 2008). Bigsten, Kimunyu, and Lundvall (2004) found that young graduates in Kenya end up picking-up apprenticeships in the *jua kali* sector (informal sector), which further attracts skilled persons who either lost formal sector jobs or were beginners in self-employment. In addition, formal-informal linkages are also demonstrated by Bigsten et al, (2004) with evidence that most of the output from the *jua kali* satisfies demand for food and other basic needs from the low- and middle-income rural and urban Kenyans. Product or service quality may be lower and prices lower than for modern sector products, but, interestingly, high quality furniture sold in the formal sector is supplied by *jua kali* enterprises.

The failure of the formal sector to generate an adequate number of jobs has meant that the informal sector continues to absorb the urban unemployed, perhaps to the relief of the polity. But this is set against another assertion that the informal sector represents a large portion of the voting bloc who the polity would wish to protect against high taxes in exchange for votes (Ayee, 2007; Di John, 2008). AfDB (2010) cites the case of Kenya, where difficulties of accessing and taxing the informal sector are attributed to populist politics, which seek to shield their constituencies in the informal sector from the tax burden, and in which case government loses revenue. A plausible resolution is to let the sector formalise, get legal status, and pay taxes.

Other than the rural-urban income differentials, the informal sector is fuelled by over-regulation - high tax rates and high cost for entering the formal sector and an inefficient and corrupt system of enforcing compliance. Arvin-Rad, Basu, and Willumsen (2010) argue that while Nelson and Bruijn (2005) attribute the increasing 'informalisation' to the lack of a formal environment, the informal economy is a response to regulations and taxes imposed on that environment.

Policy response to the positive view of the informal sector emphasises its developmental potential and the essence of reducing the cost of formalising. Different policy innovations or incentives are deployed to encourage informal operators to register and license their activities. Support includes easier access to investment and trade information, credit, improvements and enforcement of product, process and quality standards, or other business development services (OECD, 2008; Fan, Criscuolo, & Ilieva-Hamel, 2005). The scope of formalisation is extended by de Soto's (2000) advocacy of the formalisation of property rights for the workforce existing in the informal section for use as collateral.

Ayee (2007), OECD (2008), and Fosu and Drine (2009), among others, argue for an incentive mechanism through which informal sector operators get some legitimacy and enjoy public services in exchange for paying a tax. This is consistent with Di John's (2008) argument that for tax policy reform to contribute to sustainable growth it should focus on revenue generation and its relationship with the construction of productive capacities, which in turn translates into an expanded tax base of the (now) graduated firms. However, it is not assumed that payment of taxes is automatic after formalisation: an extra effort has to go into nurturing tax compliance.

## Decision to Formalise

Preference for informality is associated with the operator's tendency to avoid taxation and regulatory costs, which raise the costs of formalisation, including those related to compliance with regulations, licenses, taxes, and penalties for flouting the regulations (Dabla-Norris, Gradstein, & Inchauste, 2008). Informal sector operators will weigh the perceived benefits of formalising their activities against the possible costs of getting formal recognition and complying with current and future regulatory obligations and taxes. Formalisation costs (FC) include time and financial outlays involved in complying with regulations, payment of taxes, and risk of being convicted for non-payment of taxes or for not abiding by the regulations. The operators also weigh the costs arising from the current institutional constraints to the expansion of their business activities, such as lack of credit or property rights (Gërxhani, 2004).

In a simplified model, Nelson and Bruijn (2005) identify three decision variables for the informal operator contemplating formalising:

(i) Institutional incentives (II), which include legitimacy, rights, and benefits conferred by the legal status. Some of these benefits may be non-monetary.
(ii) Opportunity costs (OC) – potential gains lost as a result of remaining informal.
(iii) Formalisation costs (FC) – depending on the nature and location of the informal activity such cost would include the costs of preparation and processing of a license, licensing fees, taxes, time lost, and stress through the bureaucracies and costs of complying with subsequent regulations regarding health, product safety, and the environment.

The informal sector operator balances out the three variables to derive a stimulus (S) for a decision to formalise or not to formalise, that is,

(1) $S=(II+OC)-FC$

when the operator confronts high formalisation costs relative to institutional incentives and any potential gains lost as a result of not formalising, i.e.,

(2) $FC>(II+OC) \rightarrow S\downarrow$(falling) ….*avoid formalisation*

then the stimulus (S) is falling, and the informal operator will avoid formalising (2).

If the formalisation costs are lower or are falling, the informal operator will positively contemplate formalising and bear the costs (FC) (3), or

(3) $FC<(II+OC)\rightarrow S\uparrow$(rising)…*formalise.*

Ideally (3) will result in the flow of benefits to the firm. The incentives that address the informal sector's typical constraints are then expected to propel the firm's growth in terms of output and employment and for government revenue (fees and taxes).

Nelson and Bruijn (2005) are aware, however, that the three components carry unavoidable subjective elements. The final decision depends on the operator's characteristic traits such as self-confidence, disposition to risk, inclination to avoiding taxes, or a sense of moral duty towards taxes (or 'tax morale' in other studies, such as Alm & Martinez-Vazquez, 2008). Risk-averse operators confronting a situation in equation 3 may not fully embrace formalisation if, for instance, the tax policy is not stable or agents mistrust the government's commitment. Such subjective traits reduce the predictability of the operators' decisions and government's ability to precisely quantify the tax revenue it can expect to gain in return for the formalisation incentives.

Nonetheless, except for the subjective elements and the difficulty in quantifying the 'quality of regulatory systems', the model predicts that, on average, taxes and charges which tend to increase FC undermine the formalisation stimulus.

## Understanding Tax Non-compliance of the Informal Sector

Willingness to pay the tax part of the FC even at such low, presumably affordable tax rates becomes a matter of interest. First, apparently not all operators within the informal sector are unwilling to pay taxes, especially when these are in exchange for some legitimacy, stability, and protection from arbitrary harassment from state agents and if public services are provided as per social contract. For some operators, the tax burden is not onerous more than they are already paying through (say) bribes or forgone production going through the bureaucracy (Gërxhani, 2004). There are also views that tax non-compliance is not intentional, but rather from ignorance (Araujo-Bonjean & Chambas, 2003). Above all, paying taxes is as a matter of citizens' obligation in exchange for efficient public services (Quadri, 2010; Bird, 2008; Everest-Phillips, 2008).

A number of studies shed insight on the behaviour of tax payers, particularly their attitude towards tax burden and tax administration. Factors that explain non-compliance may inform the design of the tax regime for the informal sector or sub-sectors thereof. Compliance is perception based and tied to expectations and attitudes ordered differently by firms and individuals depending on how they judge fairness, trust in political institutions, governance, or institutional quality and delivery of public services; together these influence 'tax morale'. Increases in perception indicators related thereto are empirically found to reduce informality, implying positive response to paying taxes in Latin America and Europe (e.g. Alm & Martinex-Vazquez, 2008; Torgler & Schneider, 2007).

It has been possible to investigate tax compliance behaviour from single-country surveys – for instance, Marti, Wanjoh, and Magutu (2010) for Kenya and Ofori (2010) for Ghana. For Kenya, data were derived from surveys of selected businesses and areas/zones and were analysed using descriptive statistics. While for Kenya the survey sampled formal SMEs that had even the tax personal identification numbers (PINs) in a town, in Ghana, Ofori (2010) carried out a survey of informal activities that had common characteristics (food processing, textile/leather works, woodworking, metal fabricating, beverages, repair services, auto repairs, handicrafts, commerce, and building construction enterprises as 'sub-sectors') in three towns and neighbouring rural communities. The Ofori study ran tests on a number factors explaining tax non-compliance. These included the costs of compliance (related to filing procedures, time, and resources), level of knowledge about the tax liability, record keeping practices, and evasive tactics through the use of cash and changing location to avoid visibility by tax authorities. It was also investigated if the operators openly or defiantly refused to pay tax in protest against perceived unfairness of tax laws or reported abuse of tax revenue by government officials, or refused to pay as a result of peer pressure (as group or association), or refused to pay because of habitual non-compliance as a pattern of under-declaration or non-declaration.

While both the Kenya and Ghana studies are indicative of the problems to be encountered in an African country context, the Ghana study, which focused directly on informal sector activities (in contrast to the formal

SMEs study of Kenya), cautions about the extent to which information on turn-over and tax-related information can be difficult to elicit.

## 3. Reflections on Tanzania

### Formalisation

In Tanzania, the informal sector is estimated to lie between 40 and 60% of GDP: 58.2% according to Schneider (2002); about 55% according to the World Bank (2010); and 40% according to Mbilinyi (2010). Only about 400 large tax payers contribute 70% of domestic revenue collections; whereas small and medium tax payers together contribute 30% (Kitillya, 2011; Kimungu & Kileva, 2007). The country has had a persistent budget deficit (after grants) as percentage of GDP (at -4.9% in 2004/05 and -6.9% in 2010/11). Revenue effort as percentage of GDP increased, from 11.8% in 2004/05 to 17.9% in 2008/09 and was down at 15.8% GDP (2010/11) due to indirect effects of the global financial crisis. What is important for the present discussion is that the bulk of tax revenue is collected from the formal sector.

The informal sector in Tanzania has survived through the socialist regime (1960s to mid-1980s), when the informal sector was, like the formal private sector, frowned upon; it also survived administrative constraints (Swantz & Tripp, 1996; Bagachwa & Ndulu, 1996). However, during the market-oriented regime (mid-1980s to the present), it has seen more supportive policies aimed at improving the regulatory environment for SMEs and encouraging them to register (formalise). Legislation was adopted that mandates the replacement of compulsory registration and licensing with a voluntary registration approach, in which the Business Activities Registration Act (BARA) replaced the Business Licensing Act (1972). Secondly, it has been working towards a centralised registry within BRELA (World Bank, 2010).

In 2004, the Property and Business Formalisation Programme (PBFP) was introduced in order to address the main obstacles that prevent property and business owners in the informal sector from joining the formal sector. It targeted property owners in the informal sector and allowed them opportunities to use their assets to access capital and other advisory services. It had a further objective of reducing the costs of doing businesses by eliminating procedural and administrative barriers and improving the quality of services provided by the government in the private sector as well as commercial disputes resolution (URT, 2008; Sitta, 2005).

Nelson and Bruijn (2005) portray the typology of enterprise forms in Tanzania by the degree of formalisation from informal to the formal status (Table 1).

**Table 1: Description of Major Levels of Enterprise Formalisation in Tanzania**

| Status | Legal form | Description and subcategories |
|---|---|---|
| Illicit | None | Not legally permitted or registered |
| Informal | None | Activity for which there is formal counterpart, but does not comply with requirements of the regulatory system regarding licences, permits, certificates, notification or registration of the activity |
| Semi-formal | Legal authority, enterprise licensed | An operator appears on a local authority list if licensed operators but enterprise is not registered with state registrar. E.g. hawker's license and business license |
| Formal | State registered | Persons registered to conduct business activities under a registered business name – e.g. private limited company, joint stock company open to public subscription shareholdings |

Source: Nelson and Bruijn (2005), p. 580

The formal status is the highest level at which a firm is registered with the government's regulatory authority, the Business Registration and Licensing Authority (BRELA). This may occur as a voluntary action by a firm (wholly new or formerly informal) without direct pressure from government and/or out of decision to voluntarily comply with the law and avoid any future costs of non-compliance.

A lesser level of formalisation is the semi-formal status which takes place at the local authority level by applying for and obtaining an operating license. The procedures are relatively simple and the costs lower. Most operators already in the informal sector or contemplating to initiate a semi-formal status, including the better educated school (college) leavers, find this to be more approachable and a more convenient legal status to start. The semi-formal status is more amenable to taxation as long as the costs of complying with regulation and tax rates are affordable. Licensing fees are usually the main feature of the formalisation costs.

With a view to facilitating SMEs and enticing more informal sector operators to register and pay taxes voluntarily, authorities have invested in various educational programmes to promote voluntary registration, tax compliance, and enforcement strategies. Other measures include availability of tax forms, information in simple language, and accurate tax information through media, as well as an attitude of presumption of honesty on part of business unless proved otherwise (Kitillya, 2011; Luoga, 2007; TRA, 2008).

## Survey-based Studies

The Roadmap Study of the Informal Sector (ILO/UNIDO/UNDP, 2002) is one of the earliest prominent survey-based studies that report the regulatory and policy environment affecting the growth of SMEs to be a major issue in the growth of MSEs. The constraints to informal as well as formal small productive and service activities range from administrative/ bureaucratic obstructionist attitudes, long processes registering or licensing, and upfront payment of tax as part of the licensing requirement before the business has started running. Major comparative surveys highlight problems which affect the SMEs and are shared by the informal sector operators in both rural and urban areas, namely tax rates and tax administration, cost of finance, corruption, electricity, customs administration, and trading across borders (e.g. World Bank, 2004, 2006, 2008, 2010).

Madihi and Mushi (2008) conducted a survey of 667 informal operators in the trade, food processing, and woodwork sub-sectors in several cities of Dar es Salaam, including Mwanza, Mbeya, and Morogoro, where informality was defined as lack of business registration. They identified lack of awareness of the formalisation process, high costs of registration, and lack of physical premises as key obstacles to formalisation. With an attempt to estimate the unexploited potential revenue from the informal sector, URT (2010) highlights the constraints to effective assessment and collection of tax from the informal sector. While these are key insights, they do not give a clear guide on possible rates for the specific informal operators and the recommended arrangements for effectiveness remain rather general.

It may be important to take a cue from the Roadmap study as a starting point. The Roadmap categorised MSEs into 'survivalists' and entrepreneurs. Survivalists tended to want to remain small and invisible and to avoid compliance. Entrepreneurs were split again into (i) those who tended to comply in order to avoid harassment and be free to pursue their growth and (ii) those who, while pursuing their growth, refused to comply with the demands of a corrupt bureaucracy. Survivalists are not likely to respond to formalisation overtures, while entrepreneurs are likely to seek and use information about formalisation for further self-advancement. It is this category of the informal sector that should be targeted first because they are more likely to respond to formalisation overtures and messages about the essence of paying taxes.

### Exploring Tax Compliance of the Informal Sector

There are few studies on tax compliance of the informal sector in Tanzania. The general reasons for non-compliance that may apply to the informal sector analysed by Fjeldstad, Kolstad, and Nygaard (2006) include (i) the feeling by the citizens that they receive little in exchange for taxes paid in terms of services from (local) government (primary schools, water and road maintenance, law and order and the market place, garbage collection, agricultural extension services, and perceptions of corruption); (ii) oppressive and non-transparent ways of collecting taxes, fees, and charges, which tended to foster tax resistance and disrespect for the laws; and (iii) lack of access to information on taxes collected and how revenues are spent. The informal operators find themselves in constant fear and hence ready to exploit any loophole to evade or avoid the taxes.

## 4. Policy Questions and Research Agenda

### Policy Questions and Implications

The survey indicates that informal sector continues to grow and is no longer confined to its traditional definition. It can be dynamic, absorbing the unemployed, even the more educated and skilled workforce. The uptake of formalisation incentives is likely to be higher among informal sector activities that are run by the more educated and skilled workforce or the more enterprising operators, as the ILO/UNIDO/UNDP (2002) roadmap study implies. However, taxes have to be extracted not only for equity purposes, but also and more importantly to fill the fiscal gap.

Formalisation of the informal sector emerges as a key policy undertaking since it is expected to enhance the productive capacity (growth) of (in)formal sector operators and their ability to pay taxes. Once formalised the informal sector shrinks, the first follow-up question is how to quantify change or progress made through formalisation since the proposed tax is to be set on the basis of growth generated (whether on value-addition or profits). How can progress on formalisation be assessed? Is it by the number of formerly informal sector activities that have been registered between two time points? Can changes in the number of registered firms be taken as an indicator of formalisation progress? Is it not possible for changes in tax rates and tax administration to induce formalisation?

The tax strategy has to determine appropriate rates (and thresholds) and the tax administration system, preferably dedicated to the specific sub-sectors of the informal sector. It would then be important to better know the factors that influence tax compliance in that sub-sector.

Formal SMEs are still in the picture because they are the bridging stage towards large enterprises, which contribute more to tax revenue. At this level, however, the narrative proposes nothing very new except the question as to whether conceptually it is possible to have the two processes – formalisation and taxation of the informal sector – planned together. The difficulties of taxing the informal sector are not underestimated. Although Di John (2008) laments the paucity of literature that provides a clear guide to this end, this is presumably because the sector is simply heterogeneous, and the practical way to tax (as to formalise) would need to be tailored to sub-sector conditions, then sub-sector by sub-sector, a few at a time.

Examples exist of targeted tax plans for specific informal sector 'sub-sectors', such as the transport operators in Ghana (Ayee, 2007; Di John, 2007) and presumptive taxation tried and re-tried in Kenya (Moyi & Ronge, 2006), Tanzania (IFC, 2007), and elsewhere. What can be learnt from them as regards feasibility and sustainability? The transport operators' examples have an associational element, with an advantage that the tax authority can link with the operators (now more homogeneous) through the leadership of the informal operators' association. What factors determine success or failure?

It may also deliberately be decided to work with operators that are receiving formalisation support, provided they are a more homogeneous group, and determine the tax plan for and with them as Fosu and Drine (2009) and others advise. The informal sector sub-sector approach is probably the best option. Provided information is shared with the targeted sub-sector and tax education is part of the formalisation package from the start, it is possible to progressively win the trust of the enterprising operators who might then be interested in similar plans tailored to the nature of their activities.

## Possible Research Agenda

Where formalisation has been institutionalised, like in Tanzania, it is important to assess the impact and hence the efficiency of delivery of the different formalisation interventions. Tracking may be done, for instance, of old and new beneficiaries of the programme identifying those who were in the informal sector. Survey-based studies of the kind reported by Madihi and Mushi (2008) are still required for other locations, as these are informal sub-sector or area-specific and likely to yield readily usable findings on the nature and extent of different formalisation problems, tax-related concerns, and perceptions about the tax plan directed at the sub-sector level.

The need to investigate tax non-compliance is not only confined to the informal sector but also to the formal SMEs. As Ofori (2010) did for Ghana, for instance, targeting informal sector specific activities may be given priority in advance of introducing and designing a formalisation tax plans for them. Caution about the limitation of survey studies of this nature has been alluded to: many people in the informal sector tend not to volunteer information about their turnover or tax status. This kind of information may be forthcoming from a few. It means this kind of study would lead to findings that are skewed towards respondents who volunteered, but these are more likely to be entrepreneurs than survivalists. The survey can be a basis for selecting candidates for the formalisation incentives. It can safely be hoped, in theory at least, that going forward with a few entrepreneurs would set an example for later followers.

## 5. Concluding Remarks

The informal sector has generated a number of tensions. First, it has grown but is largely not paying taxes. It poses unfair competition and inequity against the tax-paying formal sector activities and formal workforce. It has also been noted that while the expansion of the sector absorbs unemployment to a large extent, to the relief of policy makers, the same informal sector expansion, by creating the 'fiscal gap' (through not paying taxes and killing the tax morale of compliant tax payers in the formal sector), undermines the policy makers' objective of expansion of the tax base. There are also confounding observations that populist politics may complicate the situation further by shielding potential tax payers in the informal sector against tax liability in order to win/protect the vote.

The positive view of the informal sector points to what is making the sector dynamic in spite of a variety of the constraints to its expansion. Innovative policies have been evolved to enable informal sector activities to overcome some or many of these constraints through formalisation incentives. The tax payment obligation of the informal sector operators, as for all citizens, must be taken along with the formalisation incentives.

## References

African Development Bank. 2010. 'Domestic Resource Mobilization for Poverty Reduction in East Africa: Kenya Case Study'. Regional Department East.

Alm, J., and J. Martinez-Vazquez. 2008. 'Tax Evasion, the Informal Sector, and Tax Morale in LAC Countries'. Andrew Young School of Policy Studies, Georgia State University.

Araujo-Bonjean, C., and G. Chambas. 2003. 'Taxing the Urban Unrecorded Economy in Sub-Saharan Africa'. Centre d'Etudes et de Recherches su le Development International (CERDI), Etudes et Documents, E 2003 16.

Arvin-Rad, H., A. K. Basu, and M. Willumsen. 2010. 'Economic Reform, Informal-Formal Sector Linkages and Intervention in the Informal Sector in Developing Countries: A Paradox'. Discussion Paper No. 5229. Bonn: The Institute for the Study of Labour (IZA).

Ayee, J. R. A. 2007. 'Building Tax Compliance through Reciprocity with Government'. Paper presented at the Foreign Investment Advisory Service (FIAS) if the World Bank Group Regional Conference on Enterprise Formalisation in Africa, Alisa Hotel, Accra.

Bangasser P. E. 2000. 'The ILO and the Informal Sector: an Institutional History'. Employment Paper 2000/9, Employment Sector, Geneva.

Barret, C. B., T., and P. Webb. 2001. 'Non-farm Income Diversification and Household Livelihood Strategies in Rural Africa: Concepts, Dynamics and Policy Implications'. Dept of Applied Economics and Management, Cornell University.

Benno, T., and F. Schneider. 2007. 'Shadow Economy, Tax Morale, Governance and Institutional Quality: A Panel Analysis'. Centre for Research in Economics, Management and the Arts, Switzerland.

Bigsten, A., P. Kimuyu, and K. Lundvall. 2004. 'What to Do with the Informal Sector?' *Development Policy Review* 22, no. 6: 701-15.

Bird, R. M. 2008. 'Tax Challenges Facing Developing Countries'. Inaugural Lecture of the Annual Public Lecture Series of the National Institute of Public Finance and Policy, New Delhi, India.

Chen, M. A. 2007. 'Rethinking the Informal Economy: Linkages with the Formal Economy and the Formal Regulatory Environment'. Economic & Social Affairs, DESA Working Paper No. 46, ST/ESA/2007/DWP/46.

Dabla-Norris, E., M. Gradstein, and M. G. Inchauste. 2008. 'What Causes Firms to Hide Output? The Determinants of Informality'. *Journal of Development Economics* 85, no. 1-2: 1–27.

Davis, J. R. 2003. 'The Rural Non-Farm Economy, Livelihoods and Their Diversification: Issues and Options'. NRI Report No. 2753, Natural Resource Institute, DFID and World Bank.

de Soto, H. 2000. *The Mystery of Capital: Why Capitalism Triumphs in the West and Fails Everywhere Else*. New York: Basic Books.

Di John, J. 2008. 'Taxation, Resource Mobilisation and Productive Capacity-Building in LDCs'. Background Paper No. 5, UNCTAD *The Least Developing Countries Report 2009*.

Engelschalk, M., and J. Loeprick. 2007. 'The Nexus of Informality and Tax Policy – Options for the Taxation of Small Enterprises in Africa'. The Multi-Donor Investment Climate Advisory Service of the World Bank Group.

Everest-Phillips, M. 2008. 'Business Tax as State-Building in Developing Countries: Applying Governance Principles in Private Sector Development'. *International Journal of Regulation and Governance* 8, no. 2: 123–54.

Fan, Q., A. Criscuolo, and I. Ilieva-Hamel. 2005. 'Whither SME Polices'. Development Outreach, World Bank Institute.

Fjeldstad O., I. Kolstad, and K. Nygaard. 2006. 'Bribes, Taxes and Regulations: Business Constraints for Micro Enterprises in Tanzania'. Chr Michelsen Institute Working Paper.

Fosu, A., and I. Drine. 2009. 'Informal Sector and Domestic Resources Mobilization'. UNU-WIDER Development Finance Network (DeFiNe) meeting, Paris, 25 September.

Gërxhani, K. 2004. 'The Informal Sector in Developed and Less Developed Countries'. Tinbergen Institute Discussion Paper, TI 1999-083/2.

Glenday, G. 2007. 'Special Regimes and Thresholds for Taxation of SMEs, International Tax Dialogue Global Conference on Taxation of SMEs'. Duke Centre for International Development and International Taxation Programme.

Gordon, A., and C. Craig. 2001. 'Rural Non-Farm Activities and Poverty Alleviation in Sub-Saharan Africa'. Policy Series 14, University of Greenwich.

Harris, J. R., and M. P. Todaro. 1970. 'Migration, Unemployment and Development: a Two-Sector Analysis'. *American Economic Review* 60, no. 1: 126-42.

International Finance Corporation (IFC). 2007. *Designing a Tax System for Micro and Small Businesses: Guide for* Practitioners. Washington, DC: International Finance Corporation/World Bank Group.

International Labour Organisation (ILO). 1972. 'Employment, Incomes and Equity: A Strategy for Increasing Productive Employment in Kenya'. Geneva: ILO.

International Labour Organisation, United Nations Development Programme, and United Nations Industrial Development Organisation. 2002. 'Roadmap Study of the Informal Sector in Mainland Tanzania Dar es Salaam'. The United Nations Development Programme (UNDP), the International Labour Organisation (ILO), and the United Nations Industrial Development Organisation (UNIDO) report.

Ingram, M., V. Ramachandran, and V. Desai. 2007. 'Why Do Firms Choose to be Informal? Evidence from the Africa Investment Climate Surveys'. Paper presented at the Africa Consultative Conference on Creating Better Business Environments for Enterprise Development, Accra, Ghana.

Islam, N. 1997. 'The Non-farm Sector and Rural Development'. International Food Policy Research Institute DP 22.

Kimungu, H. and E. L. Kileva. 2007. 'Challenges of Administering Small and Medium Taxpayers Tanzania Experience'. International Tax Dialogue Conference on SME Taxation, Buenos Aires, Argentina.

Kitillya, H. M. 2011. 'Tax Administration Reforms in Tanzania – Experience and Challenges'. Presented at the Conference on Revenue Mobilisation in Developing Countries, IMF- Fiscal Affairs Department, Washington DC.

Lewis W. W. 2004. *The Power of Productivity: Wealth, Poverty and the Thread to Global Stability*. Chicago: University of Chicago Press.

Luoga, P. 2007. 'Application of Vat to Small and Medium Size Businesses in Tanzania'. Dar es Salaam: Tanzania Revenue Authority.

Marti, L. O., M. S. Wanjoh, and O. Magutu. 2010. 'Taxpayers' Attitudes and Tax Compliance Behaviour in Kenya'. *African Journal of Business and Management* 1: 112-22.

Mbilinyi, A. 2010. 'Informal Sector Taxation in Tanzania'. Policy Brief Series No. 012-2010. Dar es Salaam: Economic and Social Research Foundation.

Moyi, E., and E. Ronge. 2006. 'Taxation and Tax Modernization in Kenya: A Diagnosis of Performance and Options for Further Reform'. Nairobi: Institute of Economic Affairs.

Müller, M. 2005. 'The Political Dynamics of the Informal Sector in Tanzania'. International Development Studies, Roskilde University Centre.

Nelson, E. G., and E. J. De Bruijn. 2005. 'The Voluntary Formalisation of Enterprises in a Developing Economy: The Case of Tanzania'. *Journal of International Development* 17: 575–93.

OECD. 2008. 'Governance, Taxation and Accountability Issues and Practices'. Paris: Organisation for Economic Co-operation and Development.

Ofori, E. G. 2009. 'Taxation of the Informal Sector in Ghana: A Critical Examination'. Dissertation for the degree of Commonwealth Executive Master of Business Administration, Institute of Distance Learning, Knust, Kumasi, Institute of Distance Learning, Kwame Nkrumah University of Science and Technology.

Palmade, V., and A. Anayiotos. 2005. 'Rising Informality'. The World Bank Group Private Sector Development Vice Presidency, Note No.298.

Quadri, K. P. R. 2010. 'Improving Voluntary Tax Compliance within the Informal Sector in Lagos State'. Presented at the 4th Lagos State Taxation Stockholders' Conference, Civic Centre, Victoria Island, Lagos.

Schneider, F. 2002. 'Size and Measurement of the Informal Economy in 110 Countries around the World'. Presented at the Workshop of Australian National Tax Centre, Australian National University.

Sitta, S. J. 2005. 'Integrity Environment and Investment Promotion-The Case of Tanzania'. Presented to the Alliance for Integrity: Government and Business Roles in Enhancing African Standards of Living Conference UN Global Compact and Transparency International, Addis-Ababa, Ethiopia.

Sookram, S., and P. K. Watson. 2008. 'Small-Business Participation in the Informal Sector of an Emerging Economy'. *Journal of Development Studies* 44: 15-31.

Stern, R. E., and P. A. Barbour. 2005. 'Designing a Small Business Tax System that Enhances Growth: Lessons from Africa'. Discussion Paper, World Bank.

Stern, R. E., and J. Loeprick. 2007. 'Small Business Taxation: Is this the Key to Formalisation? Evidence from Africa and Possible Solutions'. FIAS Tax Team, World Bank.

Swaminathan, M. 1991. 'Understanding the 'Informal Sector': A Survey'. WIDER Working Papers WP95.

Swantz, M. L., and A. M. Tripp, eds. 1996. *What Went Wrong in Tanzania? People's Response to Directed Development*. Dar es Salaam: DSM University Press.

Theis, T. 2005. 'Tanzanian Formal Sector Workers' Participation in Informal Production'. *Applied Economics* 37, no. 21: 2469-85.

Todaro, P. M., and S. C. Smith. 2009. *Economic Development*. London: Addison Wesley.

Torgler, B., and F. Schneider. 2007. 'Shadow Economy, Tax Morale, Governance and Institutional Quality: A Panel Analysis'. Centre for Research in Economics, Management and the Arts, Switzerland.

Tanzania Revenue Authority. 2008. *Third Corporate Plan 2008/09 – 2012/2013*. Dar es Salaam: TRA.

United Nations Economic Commission for Africa. 2009. 'Enhancing Domestic Resource Mobilization: Challenges and Opportunities in Southern Africa'. Lusaka: United Nations Economic Commission for Africa, 15th meeting of the Intergovernmental Committee of Experts for Southern Africa (ICE).

United Republic of Tanzania. 2008. *The Property and Business Formalisation Programme Reform Proposals*. Volume IV, Business Formalisation Reform Outlines and Packages for Mainland Tanzania Programme Management Unit.

—. 2010. 'Domestic Resource Mobilisation in Tanzania'. Consultancy Report submitted by Department of Economics, University of Dar es Salaam.

World Bank. 2004. *Investment Climate Assessment: Improving Enterprise Performance and Growth in Tanzania*. Washington, DC: World Bank/International Finance Corporation.

—. 2006. *The Rural Investment Climate: It Differs and It Matters*. Washington, DC: World Bank.

—. 2008. *The Rural Investment Climate: Analysis and Findings.* Washington, DC: World Bank, Agriculture and Rural Development Department.

—. 2010. *Better Regulation for Growth: Governance Frameworks and Tools for Effective Regulatory Reform Regulatory Capacity Review of Tanzania.* Investment Climate Advisory Services. Washington, DC: World Bank.

# SUDAN AND SOUTH SUDAN: ENSURING MUTUAL VIABILITY THROUGH MACROECONOMIC COOPERATION

ALEMAYEHU GEDA
ADDIS ABABA UNIVERSITY
AND STEVE KAYIZZI-MUGERWA
AFRICAN DEVELOPMENT BANK

*This article discusses the macroeconomic challenges and opportunities facing Sudan and South Sudan following their mutual separation in July 2011. It was written as part of the framework for informing the Sudanese and South Sudanese parties in negotiations following the secession of the South. Mutual viability was a key issue. While events have moved on since then, some of the language of the original paper has been preserved. The article argues that close economic cooperation borne out of the realisation of economic interdependence and geographical and cultural proximity should be a central feature of economic policy for both countries. Institutions to ensure this, including correspondent commercial banks and trading houses, will need to be created. Externally, Sudan and, especially the newly independent South Sudan, will need to make choices about the trading blocs to join, as well as the speed of convergence to the regional trading norms. The article concludes that Sudan-South Sudan macroeconomic cooperation could be an important agency of restraint on domestic policy makers and prevent policies from swinging too much to the vagaries of political pressure.*

## 1. Introduction[1]

The economic viability of Sudan and South Sudan, as has been underlined in their 'post-referendum negotiations', during 2011, is to a large degree, conditional on a meaningful working relationship and cooperation between the two countries on economic issues and on actions that would ensure a stable macroeconomic environment, i.e. low inflation, stable exchange rates, prudent fiscal management, and external balance. These require an overarching macroeconomic construct that incorporates negotiated solutions over a range of issues, including for example oil, other physical assets, external debt, and currency and banking. It also incorporates the theoretical and empirical bases for the discussion on economic cooperation.

Sudan and South Sudan held negotiations on oil assets, debt and currency, population movements, and rights to water and agricultural land as part of their Comprehensive Peace Agreement. The negotiations intensified in the run-up to the independence of South Sudan. The talks were guided by the common objective harboured by both Sudan and South Sudan of ensuring win-win outcomes, avoiding relapse into conflict, and ensuring the economic viability of the two states.

In this article, we argue that win-win possibilities for Sudan and South Sudan can be derived from both theoretical conjecture and practical experience: post-conflict reconstruction experiences from Africa and elsewhere indicate that there should be 'no losers if there are to be gainers'. Secondly, the equivalent conclusion in macroeconomics can be derived from the theories of optimum currency areas and those of macroeconomic cooperation: there are more benefits to cooperation than competition. Finally, the impetus of regional economic integration and the history of Sudan and South Sudan suggest that collaboration by the two will also benefit the countries' neighbours and the region as a whole.

The rest of the article is organised as follows. Section two is a brief overview of Sudan's macroeconomic performance in the five years before separation and the immediate prospects for both countries. Section three provides the analytical basis for the macro framework, based on the mutual cooperation that we are proposing. Section four lays out a set of recommendations for a framework for cooperation and looks at its institutional implications. Section five concludes the article.

## 2. Recent Macroeconomic Trends and Prospects for Sudan and South Sudan

### Major Macroeconomic Trends

Sudan was not an affluent country at independence in 1956. However, the South stood out as the poorest region, with a per capita real Gross

Domestic Product (GDP) of only about US$39, while the poorest part of the North had twice that (Ali & Elbadawi, 2004). The disparities in income have remained intact for much of the last 50 years. These have emanated from three principal differences between the South and the North. Firstly, farmers in South Sudan still depend on subsistence activities, and given the limited infrastructure, access to markets is very poor. Secondly, the stock of technologies for improving productivity in the South is not well developed, while the North has benefitted from research and agricultural outreach activities supported by the government. And, thirdly, human and institutional capacities are much more limited in South Sudan than in Sudan (World Bank, 2009; Ali & Elbadawi, 2008).

Recent data shows that during 2005–10, Sudan's economy grew by between 5–11% annually (see Table 1). This is attributable to the relative success of the country's stabilisation policies of the 1990s, its increasing access to oil revenue, and the return of peace following the signing of the Comprehensive Peace Agreement. Table 1 shows that total investment in the Sudan had reached 21% of GDP by 2010. The real exchange rate appreciated by 40% between 2005 and 2006, although depreciation during 2009 moved the Sudanese pound toward real exchange rate equilibrium by the end of the decade. Given the improvement in the financial sector, the prospects, ceteris paribus, of the macroeconomic environment in 2010 and 2011 were quite encouraging. However, the secession of the South has had important implications for the economies of both countries.

At the time of the research, there were no official sub-national GDP estimates for either Sudan or South Sudan. Based on estimates by Leo (2010) for 2009, Sudan's GDP share at the end of the decade was around 80%. That is assuming an aggregate for both countries of approximately US$54.2 billion. This implies roughly US$1,348 per capita on aggregate and US$1,361 per capita for the North and US$1,300 per capita for the South. Figure 1 further indicates the big gap between the North and South in terms of the components of GDP.

**Table 1: Selected Macroeconomic Indicators for the Sudan, 2005-2012**

| | 2005 | 2006 | 2007 | 2008 | 2009 | 2010 | 2011* | 2012* |
|---|---|---|---|---|---|---|---|---|
| Real GDP growth (%) | 6.3 | 11.3 | 10.2 | 6.8 | 6.0 | 5.1 | 4.7 | |
| GDP per capita: current US$ | 708 | 921 | 1,151 | 1,404 | 1,316 | 1,488 | 1465 | 1,986 |
| Gross Investment: as% of GDP | | 25.1 | 26.5 | 22.7 | 21.8 | 21.2 | 21.9 | 23.8 |
| Fiscal Balance: as% of GDP | | -4.0 | -3.0 | -1.4 | -5.4 | -2.9 | -3.3 | |
| Financial Depth: M2 growth rate% | 43.5 | 29.7 | 10.3 | 16.3 | 23.5 | 23.0 | 16.2 | |
| Unemployment Rate% | 17.01 | 17.49 | 16.77 | 16.04 | 14.89 | 13.73 | 12.55 | 11.36 |
| Inflation: period average% | 8.5 | 7.2 | 8.0 | 14.9 | 13.4 | 10.0 | 8.0 | 7.0 |
| Exchange Rate: Sudanese Pound/US$, end period | 2.31 | 2.01 | 2.05 | 2.18 | 2.24 | 2.78 | 2.75 | |
| Current Account Balance: as% of GDP | -10 | -13 | -10.9 | -7.7 | -10.8 | -7.7 | -7.7 | |
| FDI, net inflows: as% of GDP | 8 | 10 | 5 | 4 | 5 | | | |
| International Reserves: US$ million (In months of imports) | | 1576 | 78<br>1.4 | 1399<br>1.6 | 897<br>0.9 | 1081<br>1.0 | 1111<br>1.0 | |

Sources: World Bank World Development Indicators, International Monetary Fund (IMF) Staff Reports, and Economist Intelligence Unit.

Note: Numbers in dark italics are projections including for the two Sudans after the secession of the south. *Estimates

Figure 1: Share of Major Macro Aggregate between South and North (in percentages)

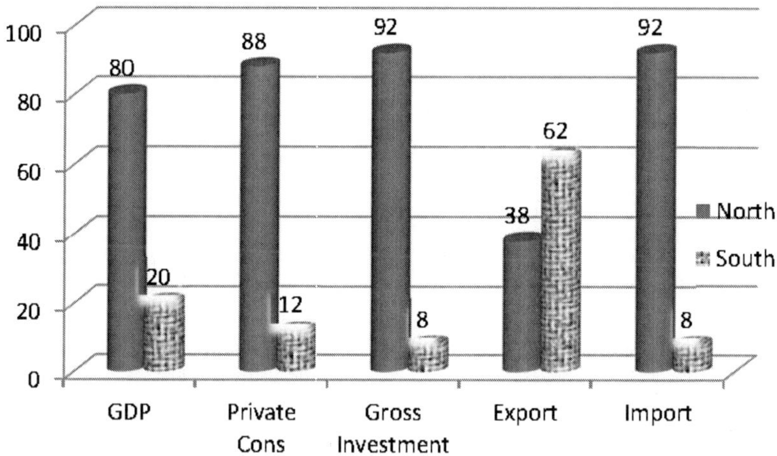


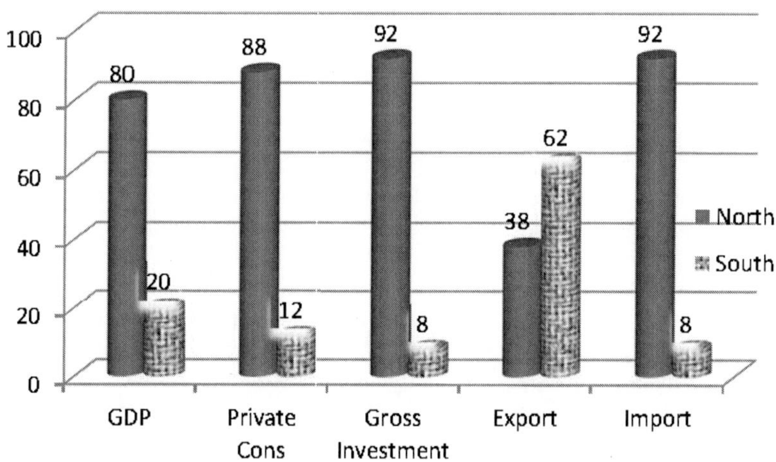


Source: Based on Leo (2010). The estimated data and breakdown is done using available information for 2009.

In terms of the structure of the economy, Sudan's growth experience since independence shows little or no economic transformation (Ali & Elbadawi, 2008). Agriculture and services accounted for 35% and 50%, respectively, of total output in 2008, while the oil sector accounted for about 10% (Abbas, Moriyama, & Naseer, 2010). This is shown in Table 2 below.

**Table 2: Structure of Sudan's GDP and Its Growth Rates, 2005-2009**

| | 2005 | 2006 | 2007 | 2008 | 2009 |
|---|---|---|---|---|---|
| Agriculture, value added: | | | | | |
| Annual percent growth | 0 | 4 | 3 | 5 | 5 |
| As percent of GDP | 32 | 30 | 28 | 26 | 30 |
| Industry, value added: | | | | | |
| Annual percent growth | 5 | 16 | 20 | 4 | 6 |
| As percent of GDP | 28 | 29 | 31 | 34 | 26 |
| Manufacturing, value added: | | | | | |
| Annual percent growth | 5 | 2 | 6 | 8 | 9 |
| As percent of GDP | 7 | 6 | 6 | 6 | 7 |
| Services, value added: | | | | | |
| Annual percent growth | 13 | 14 | 10 | 10 | 3 |
| As percent of GDP | 40 | 41 | 41 | 40 | 44 |

Source: World Bank World Development Indicators, various years.

The dominant agriculture and the oil sectors apart, the rest of the Sudanese economy was driven by small formal and informal firms. The enterprise sector as a whole consisted largely of small firms, structured as private limited companies (60%) and sole proprietorships (37%), arrayed over a wide range of sectors (United Nations Industrial Development Organisation (UNIDO), 2003). The enterprise sector was predominantly private, but a strong legacy of state participation remains. The public sector's share in GDP was nearly 40% in 2008. Small firms can be found everywhere, but larger firms are located primarily in Khartoum. Enterprises in Khartoum, Red Sea, and Gezira were, in terms of employment, bigger on average than those in the South, more capital intensive, have better educated managers and work force, and exhibit relatively higher labour productivity. Establishments in Khartoum performed better than those in the South and other states in terms of value added and sales per worker. Firms operating in Khartoum have a higher propensity to assimilate technology and to gain market competitiveness than those in other areas (World Bank, 2009). Non-managerial skills are lacking particularly in South Sudan. However, the informal sector is a large source of employment and provides an alternative service delivery mechanism (World Bank, 2009).

## The External Sector, Oil Dependence, and Macroeconomic Policy

Given the dominant role of the external sector in the economy of the Sudan (before the secession of South Sudan) and its significant influence on the macroeconomic environment both in the North and South, we have looked at the external sector in detail in the rest of this section. Sudan's total trade to GDP ratio was 44% in 2008 (World Bank, 2009) and about 36% in 2009. Net trade in goods and services fell into deficit in 2009 but was expected to return to a surplus amounting to US$1.2 billion in 2010 and US$867million in 2011, thanks to oil exports. Overall, the current account deficit—which reached some US$6 billion (10.8% of GDP) in 2009—was forecast to narrow to US$4.9 billion (7.7% of GDP) in 2010 and 7.7% of GDP in 2011 (Economist Intelligence Unit, 2010; IMF, various reports). By the end of the decade, oil accounted for about 95% of Sudan's exports (Abbas, Moriyama, & Naseer, 2010; World Bank, 2009).

Regional export and import data are not publicly available for South Sudan, owing to the difficulty of extricating it from aggregate data. However, based on estimates from 2009, the South exported the equivalent of 47% of its GDP, essentially its share of oil production. However, the North had a larger and more diversified economy and exports were only about 7% of GDP. Imports of the South equalled about 5% of its GDP, while those of the North were about 18% of GDP (Leo, 2010).

Although agricultural exports from the North are diverse, Sudan's export markets are not diversified. In South Sudan, partly owing to decades of conflict and lack of infrastructure, trade has been localized—focused predominantly on Uganda and Kenya—occurring when security conditions allow (World Bank, 2009). Trade data shows that Kenya and Uganda were exporting goods to South Sudan worth about US$75million and US$55million, respectively, in 2006. This comprised generally of manufactured goods. There was little export from South Sudan itself (World Bank, 2008). A recent World Bank survey indicates that cross border trade could be much bigger. According to the survey Uganda is the dominant exporter to South Sudan. Its exports are estimated at US$ 1.2billion per annum (the bulk of it unrecorded). Only about half a million US dollars' worth of goods are exported to Uganda from South Sudan (Yoshino, 2010).

There is a long history of cross border trade between Sudan and South Sudan. Many southerners along the border depend on food from the North, while many northern livelihoods depend on trade or access to raw materials from the South (PRI Economics Talking Points, 2011). A rapid survey of food commodity markets in South Sudan conducted in 2008 (see Ngigi, 2008) shows that the main sources of supply for major urban markets in South Sudan are Sudan itself and Uganda. According to this survey, 53% of the traders in Juba are Ugandan, while the rest are from Sudan (see also World Bank, 2009; Yoshino, 2010).

Before the secession of the South, Sudan received most of its foreign exchange from three sources: exports, Foreign Direct Investment (FDI), and private transfers (World Bank, 2009). Over the period 2005-2010, on average, oil generated 66% of foreign exchange earnings. On average, 23% of the foreign earnings are represented by FDI and 6% are private transfers, which are mostly in the form of remittances (El-Mahdi, 2010). In 2008, remittances were US$1,850 million and about 80% of remittances to the Sudan originated from developed countries. Remittances in Sudan have constituted an average of 3.5% of GDP and have increased substantially in recent years (World Bank, 2009). Sudan was the fourth largest destination for FDI in Africa in 2005, attracting US$2.3 billion (World Bank, 2009). FDI reached 10% of GDP in 2008 (Abbas, Moriyama, & Naseer, 2010). This is generally concentrated in the oil sector (El-Mahdi, 2010). With the secession of the South, Sudan experienced an 80-90% drop in net foreign earnings from oil exports.

**Table 3: Sudan's Oil, 2006-2011**

| | 2006 | 2007 | 2008 | 2009 | 2010 | 2011 |
|---|---|---|---|---|---|---|
| Oil Production (thousands of barrels per day) | 364 | 484 | 462 | 474 | *460* | 465 |
| Crude Oil Export Price: US$ per barrel | 54.4 | 58.0 | 81.3 | 47.4 | *69.1* | 72.9 |
| Oil Exports: As percent of exports | | 90.2 | 94.8 | 95.4 | 91.0 | *91.3* |
| Oil Revenues: As percent of GDP | | 11.6 | 14.3 | 7.6 | 8.0 | 8.8 |

Sources: IMF Staff Report 2010 and Staff-Monitored Program for 2009-10.

Note: Numbers in italics are projections.

As shown in Table 3, Sudan's economy became highly dependent on the oil sector, especially the world price of oil (Abbas, Moriyama, & Naseer, 2010). In 2010, Sudan had a production capacity of about 485,000 barrels per day and oil exports constitute above 90% of the country's total exports (about 8% of GDP). There was a monopolistic and direct role for the government in all phases of the oil industry. This is shrouded with limited transparency (World Bank, 2009). The majority of the estimated five billion barrels of proven oil reserves are located in the Muglad and Melut basins in the South (Energy Information Administration, 2009). South Sudan continues to be dependent on Khartoum for all oil transport and exportation (Leo, 2010). Although most oil production is in the South, refining infrastructure is based in the North. Southern crude oil is transported by pipeline, about 800 kilometres long, to the refinery in Khartoum or for direct export via Port Sudan. Finished products are then shipped to demand centres in the South. Sudan's consumption of oil products has been growing rapidly but oil demand in the South Sudan is currently quite small, which reflects low income levels and the lack of infrastructure (World Bank, 2009).

Sudan's dependence on oil exports has had important implications for the economy. In 2008, according to IMF, oil represented 60% of government revenues and 95% of export revenues. For South Sudan, oil represented 98% of total revenues. This is compared to Sudan's figure of 65% (Energy Information Administration, 2009). At current levels of production and oil reserve levels, revenues from oil in Sudan will run out in 20 to 30 years. Oil production will peak by 2012 in the most optimistic scenario (World Bank, 2009). This will have implications for external debt (the stock of public and publicly guaranteed debt), which stood at US$38 billion in 2010. Sudan has experienced mounting public debt and accumulation of arrears. Sudan's total debt is projected to reach US$40 billion by the 2011/12 fiscal year. Debt has more than doubled since 2000. An important implication of the Sudan's extreme dependence on oil as a source of foreign exchange, proven following the military confrontations between the two Sudans, is the vulnerability to external shocks. This has severe effects on fiscal revenues and the exchange rate.

In sum, the advent of an oil-based economy and sharp fluctuations in global commodity prices have presented key macroeconomic challenges for policymakers in Sudan and South Sudan—from how to prevent the economy from overheating to finding ways to maintain growth. Two key characteristics have defined Sudan's fiscal management of the oil revenue boom—although revenue streams are subject to fluctuations, absorption has been nearly complete, without savings to enable expenditure smoothing by the public sector. Volatility was thereby transferred wholly to expenditures (World Bank, 2009).

Looking ahead, managing oil revenue will be critically important in South Sudan, where dependence on oil revenues is more extreme and expenditure volatility is more severe than in Sudan (World Bank, 2009). This new challenge for macroeconomic management was accentuated by the secession of the South. There is much to gain in adopting a more collaborative policy framework. We shall explore these issues in much more detail in the rest of the article.

## Macroeconomic Challenges for Sudan and South Sudan during the Transition Period and Beyond

Given the macroeconomic posture and prospects for Sudan and South Sudan, what are the likely challenges for both countries during the 'transition period' and beyond? This is where 'transition period' is understood to be the period during which Sudan and South Sudan will reach a set of agreements over a range of issues, including oil assets and external debt.

During the 'transition period', we postulated that Sudan will encounter the following challenges: The first challenge is loss of oil revenue. The IMF projected that Sudan could lose up to 75% of its oil (export) revenue during the transition period. Given that oil revenue constitutes about 60% of government revenue and 90% of exports, this has had implications for both internal and external balance. Second, the independence of South Sudan implies a reduction by 20% of Sudan's total GDP, as shown in Figure 1.[2] It will lead to a decline in imports of goods and services given the decline in foreign currency earnings. Investment and investment income may also decline. Finally, imports of petroleum will increase during the transition period as stocks are depleted. However, in turn, it will have free resources previously allotted to transportation, port storage, and processing capacities for petroleum destined to South Sudan. On the other hand, there might be no natural alternative uses for the freed capacities, including employees, and these might remain idle.

The combined macroeconomic effects of the above consist of (based on IMF estimates): a drop in government oil revenue of 50 to 75%

(equivalent to 4 to 6% of GDP). Even after taking into account the offsetting effect of ending transfers to South Sudan during the transition period, Sudan's fiscal deficit may still widen by about 2 to 3% of GDP, unless additional spending cuts are introduced. Similarly, Sudan's current account could deteriorate by about 4% of GDP annually. This implies a current account deficit of about 10 to 12% of GDP in the medium term. Finally, capital flows such as FDI are expected to decline owing both to location of oil fields in the South and the general uncertainty associated with the transition period. This will lead to a financing gap of about 3 to 4% of GDP.

Thus, the most important macroeconomic challenge in Sudan is to maintain low inflation and a stable exchange rate in the face of these fundamental and permanent shocks that will raise the fiscal deficit and worsen the balance of payments. These may in turn threaten growth, reverse poverty reduction and social cohesion, and disrupt peace.

The most important challenge for South Sudan is managing the spill over effects of the macroeconomic challenges faced by Sudan noted above (which could amount to economic depression in the North). Given the strong historical links between the two economies, and limited macroeconomic policy tools and capacity to manage them at the disposal of South Sudan, all the economic challenges of Sudan will be of concern for South Sudan. In the South, nearly 51% of the population lives below the poverty line, with very limited infrastructure, and with a large share of basic services being provided by non-governmental organisations (NGOs). South Sudan was at the same time confronted by an ongoing need for post-conflict reconstruction.

The macroeconomic challenge for South Sudan is thus basically how to create conditions that enhance business opportunities and other livelihoods for the population and how to fulfil the expectation of a peace dividend from the different groups in the South. The major constraints to address these macroeconomic challenges are, and will continue to be, shortage of human and institutional capacities, resource constraints, and lack of domestic absorptive capacity, even when assistance comes from the international community. Other challenges include lack of macroeconomic policy instruments to tackle external shocks (at least during the transition), low macroeconomic management capacity (including fiscal discipline), and the possibility of a 'Dutch Disease' problem (that is the overheating of the economy and associated effects of 'easy money')[3] as more oil resources flow to the South.

The constraints outlined above will generally manifest themselves in the difficulty of maintaining low fiscal deficits, low inflation, and stable exchange rates. This will have implications for reaping of the expected peace dividend and how it is shared among South Sudan's regions and counties, as well as between the state and the civil society.

While each of the two new countries is expected to address these challenges individually, their respective efforts need to be accompanied by a joint macroeconomic cooperation framework so that the common goals are not thwarted by each country's individual actions in pursuing its individual national interest. A cooperative framework is not only optimal, as it provides a win-win outcome for the countries, but also a guarantee to avoid a relapse into conflict, while strengthening economic integration between the two countries.

## 3. Analytical Framework and Lessons for the Two Sudans

### Lessons from the Theories of Macroeconomic Cooperation and Optimum Currency Area

The impetus for macroeconomic policy harmonisation comes from the link between the fiscal deficit, exchange rate, and the external sector. The latter two are the channels through which a country is linked with the rest of the world. Facilitating such a link is crucial for successful regional integration or the viability of the two states that just emerged from conflict. This cooperation will have the following benefits, outlined below.

First, the optimum currency area theory asserts that a small open economy such as South Sudan will gain from joining a larger currency area so as to reduce transaction costs and exploit economies of scale, as well as avoid disruption in trade. Empirical evidence shows that a currency union leads to higher bilateral trade. Thus, dissolution of currency unions could reduce bilateral trade by at least half (Glick & Rose, 2000). Second, macroeconomic cooperation promotes trade and ensures more synchronised cycles between partners. Moreover, a macroeconomic cooperation and optimum currency area formulation has the advantages of: firstly, avoiding speculative capital; secondly, requiring less need for high levels of exchange reserves; and, thirdly, encouraging integration of economies and integration of policy.

These benefits of cooperation, however, are not without costs. The most important cost being a possible lack of policy instruments to handle external shocks, in particular when the shocks are asymmetric or are symmetric but have asymmetric effects. For instance, if the two countries agree on a fixed exchange rate, and there is lack of macroeconomic policy coordination, which may lead one party, Sudan, say, to follow fiscal expansion, South Sudan would tackle the implied contraction of its economy by exchange rate (monetary) policy, such as devaluation. However, that would be ruled out by the fixed exchange agreement. This underscores the need for macroeconomic policy harmonisation, which in this case would be an agreeable fiscal policy stance. Another possible cost is the constraint that the macro-cooperation puts on national fiscal policy. Such limitations on using macro policy may lead to unemployment if a country with low inflation and balance of payment surplus unites with one that has an opposite macro stance, as the latter needs to tighten macro policy to converge with its partner.

Despite the possibilities of such costs, theory asserts that the benefits of cooperation outweigh the costs as long as macro policy harmonisation is properly adhered to. Reaping these benefits of macroeconomic cooperation is, however, conditional on the following issues. First, the spill over effect of one country's macro policy on the other country depends on the exchange rate regime, degree of capital inflow, and wage-price mechanism (flexible or not) in both countries. In particular, if factors of production such as labour and capital are not mobile (flexible) between the two regions and countries, to adjust any disequilibrium that may emerge from external shocks, breaking away from the monetary union to get exchange rate as a monetary policy instrument might be the only option (Mundel, 1961). Thus, labour and capital mobility negotiations need to be linked with macro policy negotiations. Second, to benefit from the macro policy cooperation and the currency union during a transition period and beyond, which is similar to the optimum currency area's theoretical conjecture, the following conditions need to be noted (De Grauwe, 2007; Gandolfo, 2002):

a) First, a smooth macroeconomic cooperation is effective when there is symmetry of shocks. This is relevant for the two Sudans as shocks may fundamentally come from the oil price change. It is necessary that such shocks will not result in asymmetric impacts in the two Sudans.

b) Second, the higher the openness, the higher the benefits of macroeconomic cooperation. It helps countries avoid disruptions to the non-traded sector and abates any resultant inflation following, say, a balance of payments deficit and the consequent depreciation, since, de facto, the two economies are still open to each other. This is conducive for macroeconomic cooperation.

c) Third, high financial and trade integration also helps avoid huge changes in the exchange rate. Since Sudan and South Sudan were one country until recently, maintaining a close economic relationship is a condition for success in policy cooperation.

d) Fourth, convergence in the rate of inflation in Sudan and South Sudan is necessary to benefit from macro policy cooperation. Disparity in inflation on the other hand calls for changing exchange rate to correct disequilibria. This policy instrument cannot be used in the transition period and beyond since a common currency or a pegged relation between the new and old currency will prevail during that period.

e) Fifth, a country with diversified exports is more likely to afford a fixed exchange rate, and hence the benefits of macroeconomic cooperation, than a mono export economy. Thus, a policy of diversification in both Sudan and South Sudan is crucial for success in macro policy cooperation, although this is a long run issue.

f) Finally, macro policy coordination is necessary to minimise the impact of policies in one country that may generate shocks or macro spill-overs (such as fiscal deficits) on the other country.

## Lessons from Africa's Regional Integration and Post-Conflict Reconstruction Experiences

In most post-conflict economies, the major cause of conflict is grounded in the political economy of the country. The following four features abound during post-conflict reconstruction (see Ajaikiye & Ali, 2009). The first is a planning framework with a fairly long-time horizon and an overarching objective of poverty reduction; the second is that social policy-making in such countries is usually different from that in non-conflict countries; the third is that overcoming the disruptions of conflict requires a high volume of aid flows, but with implications on the effectiveness of aid in a period at the beginning of recovery of low absorptive capacity; and the fourth is that interventions need to be preceded by a deeper understanding of African societies. With these guiding principles, the reconstruction in Sudan and South Sudan need to focus on the following core areas, especially relevant in post-conflict and fragile states (see Alemayehu 2011):

a) The first core area relates to the immediate needs of post-conflict states, or capacity building to provide humanitarian assistance, which includes conflict-related emergency relief, and demobilisation, as well as related social services. This should be based on a wider development framework that would facilitate a rapid transition from emergency to development.

b) The second relates to the need to address the core economic and political causes of conflict, which includes the transformation of the economy as well as engaging in economic activities with a high propensity to create jobs for the young and the unemployed, who are predisposed to a life of crime and violence. This also includes building institutions that ensure peaceful power sharing mechanisms. This political aspect of post-conflict reconstruction is linked with economic reconstruction, and both should be tackled simultaneously.

c) The third relates to the issues of financing and financial sector reconstruction. Two issues are important here: the first one relates to the construction of the financial sector itself (including its regulation), without which there might be a relapse into conflict. The second one relates to the issue of financing the post-conflict reconstruction by international financial agencies and donors; particularly important tasks include currency reform, rebuilding the functions of central banks, revitalising the banking sector, and strengthening prudential supervision and regulation.

In addition to their post-conflict status, Sudan and South Sudan will also be part of one or more of Africa's regional communities. Thus, it is important to inform the proposed macroeconomic cooperation framework of the two by drawing on lessons from the experience of these regional integration schemes.

Envisioning both countries as members of the Common Market for Eastern and Southern Africa (COMESA), the East African Community (EAC), and/or the Inter-Governmental Authority on Development (IGAD) would ease the challenge of macroeconomic cooperation proposed in this article, which is based on convergence criteria adopted by such regional integration schemes. However, integration schemes in Africa, COMESA and IGAD included, are besieged by many problems, and the two countries need to pay special attention to the following outstanding challenges to facilitate their macroeconomic cooperation. In this regard the lessons from integration challenges in Africa include the following (see Alemayehu & Haile, 2008):

a) First, that tariff revenue is one of the most significant sources of government revenue. The cooperation between the two may entail revenue loss. This complicates the inter-temporal trade-off between the short-term loss of revenue and the expected long-term benefits emanating from regional integration. They need to note this in the design of their cooperation agreement.

b) Second, compensation issues and variations in initial conditions, which relate to the issue of appropriate mechanism to ensure that gainers would compensate losers in the short run and losses are minimised in the long run. The Sudan and South Sudan need to deal with this issue if one party is found to benefit unduly from the proposed cooperation framework.

c) Third, the issue of private sector participation, as it is important to create the right conditions for the participation of the private sector, as well as the public at large. To do this successfully requires a good amount of policy transparency and accountability.

To address these important impediments to regional integration, development partners of Sudan and South Sudan should assist by supporting their entry into regional programmes, such as those for regional infrastructure provision, trade, and sector diversification. Already South Sudan is in the process of joining the East African Community, and Sudan has also applied to join.

# 4. Framework for Economic Cooperation

## Targets for Macroeconomic Cooperation and Convergence Criteria

Our analysis of the macroeconomic conditions and prospects has shown that both Sudan and South Sudan will be extremely vulnerable to external shocks, especially related to the international oil market. Macroeconomic cooperation between Sudan and South Sudan will be necessary to avoid relapse into conflict and ensure the viability of the two economies. It will also generate a win-win situation for both countries. Based on the road map of a regional economic community, COMESA, to which Sudan is a member and South Sudan could be a member, the following macroeconomic targets are suggested to ensure macroeconomic stability in the two countries (see Table 4). Adhering to these targets is a necessary condition for macroeconomic stability in both countries, with the details worked out between countries.

Apart from monetary policy that may be widely used in the context of managing external shocks, there is need for fiscal policy coordination. Fiscal policy action of one country may have macro spill overs through income, spending, inflation, and borrowing costs on the other country. The level of sustainable debt in each of the countries is also linked to budget deficits. Thus, a broader agreement on fiscal policy coordination is an important issue for macroeconomic cooperation. Fiscal policy harmonisation can also serve as a restraint, enforcing fiscal discipline.

There is also a need to understand clearly the implications of South Sudan's independence and the agreement on currency for trade between the two countries. Empirical studies suggest that trade between countries in the same currency area (such as the Sudanese Pound) is three times higher than trade outside such a framework—this is called the Rose effect (Rose, 2000). Even a very pessimistic scenario shows that trade in currency areas is at least 50% higher than in otherwise similar situations. The implication of a currency agreement for trade and growth between the two countries needs to be an essential part of a macroeconomic cooperation framework.

The two countries also need to agree on tackling the emerging problem of managing resources from the booming oil sector (the Dutch Disease problem) as well as the streamlining and harmonisation of trade, including boarder trade, between the two countries. Trade with other neighbouring countries such as Uganda (for South Sudan) will make the task of policy makers even more challenging. Once an agreement on broader macroeconomic targets such as those outlined in Table 4 are made, there is a need to accompany such an agreement by an identification of the required or implied institutional arrangements for their implementation. This is briefly discussed in the next section.

**Table 4: A Macroeconomic Cooperation Targets for Sudan and South Sudan**

| Macroeconomic Criteria | COMESA | | Current Status of the Sudan | | Suggested Target for the Transition Period [&] |
|---|---|---|---|---|---|
| | COMESA Owen Criteria (2011-2015) | Adopted Maastricht Criteria | 2009 | 2010 | |
| COMESA Primary Criteria | | | | | |
| Inflation | < 3% | < 3% | 11% | 11% | <7% ** |
| Budget Deficit to GDP ratio (excluding grants) | < 5% | < twice lowest in COMESA | -4.6% | -2.7% | COMESA |
| Central banks finance of the budget deficit (% GDP) | eliminate | n/a | 2.3% | 1.2% | 2% (Average) |
| External reserves (in month of imports) | 4 month | 5 months | 0.9 | 1.0 | 4 or 5*** |
| COMESA Secondary Criteria | | | | | |
| Exchange rate stability /period for EU | To be achieved and maintained | 3 years, against US $ | | | COMESA |
| Market based positive real interest rate | To be achieved and maintained | | | | COMESA |

| | | | | | |
|---|---|---|---|---|---|
| Achievement and maintenance of real GDP growth rate | 7% or more | | 6% | 5.1% | COMESA |
| External Debt (% of GDP) | < 50% or Sustainable level | < 60% | 64% | 58.8% | COMESA |
| Domestic Revenue to GDP ratio | 20% | > 10% | 15.4% | 16% | COMESA |
| Current account deficit (excluding grants) (% of GDP) | Sustainable level | n/a | -12% | -9.3% | >-10% |
| Achievement and maintenance of domestic investment rate | At least 20% | | 21.7 | 21.2 | COMESA |
| 25 core principles of bank supervision and regulation based on agreed action plan for harmonisation of bank supervision for the COMESA | To be implemented | | | | COMESA |
| Core principles of systematically important payment systems, by modernizing the payment and settlement system | To be adhered to | | | | COMESA |
| Broad money growth | < 10%* | n/a | 23.5% | 23% | COMESA |
| Capital account liberalization | Gradual | Fully liberalized | | | COMESA |

Source: ECA (2008). Assessing Regional Integration in Africa (ARIA III). Addis Ababa: Economic Commission for Africa (ECA).

Note: Values with * and the column 'Adopted Maastricht Treaty' is based on Alemayehu (2001); n/a=not available *** SADC and Adopted Maastricht rate of COMESA.

** Average of COMESA target and recent (2009 to 2010) level of inflation in the Sudan being the floor and single digit target being the ceiling. The transition period loosely refers to the period that will see the end of current negotiated agreements at least on oil and currency (perhaps on debt too), with a view to having two viable economies.

## Institutional Requirements for Macroeconomic Cooperation

Each of the steps in macroeconomic coordination may entail different levels of institutional development (Zahler, 2001). The two countries were a unitary state not long ago and do not have to go through the long process of learning macroeconomic coordination. Notwithstanding that, there will be a tension between surrendering the sovereignty of policy making and the gain that could be obtained from macro policy coordination when a country splits into two sovereign nations. It is therefore logical to expect such tension between Sudan and South Sudan, especially given the history of conflict between the two. The following macro and institutional imperatives are required for successful macroeconomic cooperation:

a) The first imperative is that macro policy coordination will require an institutional set-up for evaluating and monitoring the agreed upon policy measures such as the convergence criteria suggested in Table 4. This may require an elaborated institutional set up and an effective surveillance mechanism.

b) The second is that once the institutional frameworks for harmonisation of macro policies are established, the next task is to agree on the suggested major convergence criteria (Table 4) and ensure their implementation. This requires working on surveillance mechanisms aimed at monitoring progress towards the agreed upon targets. This needs to be backed by enforcement mechanisms to ensure adherence to the convergence criteria.

c) The third is that the cooperation framework between Sudan and South Sudan will be feasible only if the two parties agree to deal with asymmetry of shocks when they emerge during the course of their cooperation period. Given their economic structure, both are vulnerable to external shocks that may come from the global oil market, although to differing degrees. Asymmetry of shocks (or effects) and their policy implications could be a major constraint on macro policy harmonisation for both. Full macroeconomic coordination under such asymmetries reinforces the need for compensatory funds and sharing of fiscal adjustment costs (see Vos, 2001).

d) The fourth is that establishing the institutional framework for macro policy harmonisation and maintaining the surveillance mechanism to monitor the convergence criteria require the surrender of a degree of autonomy in domestic policy making, establishing an elaborate and transparent institutional mechanism (or harness the existing ones), designing feasible convergence criteria (or agree on suggested ones), and having an effective surveillance mechanism.

e) The fifth is that the two countries may learn from the 'Stability and Growth Pact' of the European Union, the principle of 'fiscal federalism', and the 'Subsidiary Principle'[4] to establish the institutional framework for realising macroeconomic cooperation between themselves.

f) Finally, there is a need for human capacity development to undertake rigorous economic analysis and surveillance, accompanied by effective macro policy coordination between Sudan and South Sudan. These in turn presume a good vision and political commitment. The latter has not been abundant in recent months, since the independence of South Sudan.

## 5. Conclusion

This article states the case for macroeconomic policy collaboration between Sudan and South Sudan as a strategy for the mutual viability of the two states even after the secession of the South from the North. On the face of it, separation and independent development might appear to be the option to pursue for countries that have had a history of mutual animosity and whose relationship has been characterised by decades of conflict and disagreement. This atmosphere has continued even after the independence of the South, even as both countries continue to underline the importance, indeed inevitability, of collaboration.

However, with a long common border, history of economic links (including oil), and populations straddling their common border, economic and political collaboration must continue to be pursued. Therefore, looking ahead, there will be need to develop institutions to support macroeconomic collaboration and to implement the criteria agreed between the two parties to reach their mutual goals. The article has given an example of the COMESA criteria after which the countries could strive.

With the support of the international community, the two Sudans have made progress in their negotiations on several areas related to peaceful co-existence. However, viable macroeconomic collaboration will require more frequent bilateral and often low key agreements between the countries on how to proceed. More broadly, macroeconomic collaboration between the two Sudans augurs well for the region. Conflict has held back development regionally, as poor neighbourhoods hinder both foreign and domestic investment in the whole region. More collaborative and peaceful development for the Sudans will thus have a positive effect for the whole region.

## Notes

[1] This article is an extract from a longer Background Paper written by Alemayehu Geda (Addis Ababa University) for the African Union High Level Implementation Panel that is coordinating peace talks and related issues between Sudan and South Sudan, supported by the African Development Bank. The paper was first presented in February-March 2011 at the meeting of the negotiating Parties from Sudan and South Sudan in Debre Zeit, Ethiopia. Economists of the African Development Bank's Regional Department II for East Africa and the African Union (AU) Panel (OREB) have made extensive comments and suggestions for improvements on the paper, and we thank them all. Addis Yimer formatted the paper, and we are grateful for that.

[2] Although the people in South Sudan move with their GDP share, there could be loss for Sudan, among other things, in terms of tax and non-tax revenue: loss for lack of scale economies and loss from the structure of distribution of income, as well as absolute decline in national income.

[3] Invariably, following the discovery of oil there follows a rise in government spending (especially in the non-traded sector) that leads to appreciation of the real exchange rate and hence hurting traditional exports. Governments could also lose incentive to collect taxes. This is usually referred as the 'Dutch Disease' problem (see Alemayehu, 2013).

[4] The *Stability and Growth Pact* is the institutional framework to implement the 3% of GDP budget deficit criteria for admission to the European monetary union. It consists in a definition of excess deficit; has a preventive arm to prevent going to excess deficit and a corrective arm that sanction when the limit is breached. *Fiscal federalism* applied in this case allows for jointly imposing discipline in the case of externalities and increasing return possibilities. It also allows for retaining sovereignty when there is heterogeneity of preferences and information asymmetry. The principle of *subsidiarity* says that the burden of proof lies with those who argue in favour of sharing sovereign tasks.

## References

Abbas, A., K. Moriyama, A. and Naseer. 2010. 'Fiscal Adjustment in Sudan: Size, Speed, and Composition'. IMF Working Paper n0. WP/10/79. Washington, DC: International Monetary Fund.

Alemayehu, Geda. 2001. 'Fiscal Policy Harmonisation in the Context of African Economic Integration'. A Study Prepared for Regional Economic Cooperation and Integration Division (RCID) of the Economic Commission for Africa, ECA.

—. 2002. *Finance and Trade in Africa: Macroeconomic Response in the World Economy Context*. London: Palgrave-Macmillan.

—. 2008. 'A Review of Global Macroeconometric Models'. Addis Ababa, Ethiopia: Commission for Africa.

—. 2011. 'Capacity Building in Fragile and Post-Conflict States in Africa'. *World Journal of Entrepreneurship, Management and Sustainable Development* 7. No. 2-4.

—. 2013. 'The Macroeconomics of Commodity Boom in Africa'. Background Paper. Harare, Zimbabwe: African Capacity Building Foundation.

Alemayehu, Geda and Haile, Kibret. 2008. 'Regional Economic Integration in Africa: A Review of Problems and Prospects with a Case Study of COMESA'. *Journal of African Economies* 17, no. 3: 257-394.

Ali, Ali Abdel Gadir and Ibrahim A. Elbadawi. 2008. 'Explaining Sudan's Economic Growth Performance'. In *The Political Economy of Growth in Africa: 1960-2000, Country Case Studies*, ed. Benno J. Ndulu, Stephen A. O'Connell, Jean-Paul Azam, Robert H. Bates, Augustin K. Fosu, and Jan Willem Gunning. Cambridge: Cambridge University Press.

Aryeetey, E. 2000. 'Regional Integration in West Africa'. Paper Presented at A Policy Workshop organised by the OECD Development Center at the Graduate Institute of International Studies, Geneva, Switzerland.

Balassa, Bela. 1983. 'Policy Response to External Shocks in Sub-Saharan African Countries'. *Journal of Policy Modeling* 5 no. 1: 75-105.

Baldwin, Richard and Charles Wyplosz. 2006. *The Economics of European Integration*. London: McGaw-Hill.

Braun, M., R. Hausmann, and L. Pritchett. 2002. *The Proliferation of Sovereigns: Are There Lessons for Integration?* Cambridge: Harvard University Press.

Capek, A. 1992. 'The Past and the Future of Czecho-Slovak Economic Relations'. Working Paper Series no 22. Program on Central and Eastern Europe.

De Gauwe, Paul. 1997. *The Economics of Monetary Integration.* Oxford: Oxford University Press.

—. 2007. 'On Monetary and Political Union'. Paper prepared for the CESifo Workshop on 'Enlarging the Euro Area', Munich, Germany.

Economic Commission for Africa. 2007. 'Assessing Regional Integration in Africa (ARIA III)'. Addis Ababa: Economic Commission for Africa.

Economist Intelligence Unit. 2010. 'Country Report Sudan September 2010'. London: The Economist Intelligence Unit Limited.

Elbadawi, Ibrahim. 1997. 'The Impact of Regional Trade and Monetary Scheme on Intra-Sub-Saharan African Trade'. In *Regional Integration and Trade Liberalization in Sub-Saharan Africa: Framework, Issues and Methodological Perspectives*, ed. A. Oyejide, I. Elbadawi, and P. Collier. London: Macmillan.

El-Mahdi, A. 2010. 'Post-Referendum Economic Challenges Focusing on Northern Sudan'. Energy Information Administration (2009). Sudan Country Analysis Brief. http://www.eia.doe.gov.

European Institute for Security Studies. 2009. 'Post-2011 Scenarios in Sudan: What Role for the EU'. ISS Report No. 06, November.

Felgenhauer, T. (n.d.) 'Ukraine, Russia and the Black Sea Fleet Accords'. WWS Case Study 2/99.

Fidrmuc, J. and J. Fidrmuc. 2001. 'Disintegration and Trade'. Discussion Paper 99/2001. Belgium: LICOS Centre for Transition Economics.

Fidrmuc, J. and J. Horvath. 1998. *Stability of Monetary Unions: Lessons from the Break-up of Czechoslovakia.* Center for Economic Research.

Frenkel, J. A. and A. Razin. 1996. *Fiscal Policies and Growth in the World Economy.* Cambridge: Massachusetts Institute of Technology Press.

Gandolfo, Giancarlo. 2002. *International Finance and Open Economy Macroeconomics.* Heidelberg: Springer Publishing.

Goldstein, Morris. 1994. 'Improving Economic Policy Coordination: Evaluating some new and some not-so-new Proposals'. In *The International Monetary System*, ed. P. B. Kenen, Francesco Papadia, and Fabrizio Saccomanni. Cambridge: Cambridge University Press.

Government of Southern Sudan. 2010. 'GOSS Growth Strategy 2010-2012'. Juba: Government of South Sudan

—. 2011. 'Government of Southern Sudan 2011 Budget Speech'. Juba: Government of South Sudan.

Hallwod, C. Paul and Ronald MacDonald. 2000. *International Money and Finance.* Third Edition. London: Blackwell Publishing.

Hasani, E. 2006. 'The Evolution of the Succession Process in Former Yugoslavia'. *Thomas Jefferson Law Review* 29, no. 111.

IMF. 2009. 'Sudan: Staff-Monitored Program for 2009-10'. Washington, DC: IMF.

—. 2010. 'Sudan: Article IV Consultation–Staff Report; Debt Sustainability Analysis; Staff Statement; Public Information Notice on the Executive Board Discussion; Statement by the Executive Director'. Washington, DC: IMF.

Leo, Benjamin. 2010. 'Sudan Debt Dynamics: Status Quo, Southern Secession, Debt Division, and Oil—A Financial Framework for the Future', Working Paper No 233. Washington, DC: Center for Global Development.

Linn, J. 2004. 'Economic (Dis)Integration Matters: The Soviet Collapse Revisited'. Paper Prepared for a Conference on 'Transition in the CIS: Achievements and Challenges', September 13-14, Academy for National Economy, Moscow, Russia.

Masson, Paul. 2001 'Fiscal Policy and Growth in the Context of European Integration'. IMF Working Paper no. WP/00/133. Washington, DC: IMF.

Masson, Paul and Catherine Pattilo. 2001. 'Monetary Union in West Africa: An Agency of Restraint for Fiscal Policies?' IMF Working Paper no. WP/01/34, Washington, DC: IMF.

McKinnon, Ronald. 1963. ''Optimum Currency Areas'. *American Economic Review* 53: 717–25.

Mundell, Robert. 1961. ''Theory of Optimum Currency Areas'. *American Economic Review* 51: 657–65.

NCP Economic Team. 2011. 'Talking Points and Questions'. African Union Panel, NCP Economic Team Brief.

Ndung'u, Njuguna. 2000. 'Regional Integration Experience in Eastern Africa Regions'. Paper Presented at a policy workshop organised by the OECD Development Center at the Graduate Institute of International Studies, Geneva, Switzerland.

Ngigi, Margaret. 2008 'Structure, Conduct and Performance of Commodity Markets in South Sudan: Linkages Food Security'. Famine Early Warning Systems Network (FEWS NET), South Sudan Office.

O'Connell, Stephen. 1997 'Macroeconomic Harmonisation, Trade Reform and Regional Trade in Sub Saharan Africa'. In *Regional Integration and Trade Liberalization in Sub-Saharan Africa: Framework, Issues and Methodological Perspective*, ed. Ademola Oyejide, Ibrahim Elbadawi, and Paul Collier. London: Macmillan.

Oates, Wallace E. 1999. 'An Essay on Fiscal Federalism'. *Journal of Economic Literature* 37: 1120-1149.

Olszanski, T. 2001. *Ukraine and Russia: Mutual Relations and the Conditions That Determine Them.* CES Studies.

Pirani, S. 2010. 'How Post-Soviet Transition and Economic Crises Shaped the Russo-Ukrainian "Gas Wars"'. Paper for the PEEER Seminar 'Governing Energy in Europe and Russia', September 3-4, Oxford Institute for Energy Studies.

Pirani, S., J. Stern, and K. Yafimava. 2009. 'The Russo-Ukrainian Gas Dispute of January 2009: A Comprehensive Assessment'. Oxford Institute for Energy Studies.

PRI Economics Talking Points. 2011. 'Economic Inter-Linkages between Northern and Southern Sudan: Talking Points'. African Union Panel. Public International Law Yugoslav Agreement on Succession Issues (2001).
http://www.dipublico.com.ar/.../Yugoslav-agreement-on-succession-issues-2001.

Rose, Andrew. 2000. 'One Money, One Market: The Effect of Common Currencies on Trade'. *Economic Policy* 30: 9–45.

Rowlands, D. 1997. 'International Aspects of the Division of Debt under Secession: The Case of Quebec and Canada'. *Canadian Public Policy* 23, no. 1.

Smidkova, K. (n.d.). 'Costs and Benefits of Monetary Disintegration: The Czech-Slovak Case'. Prague: Czech National Bank.

Stanic, A. 2001. 'Financial Aspects of State Succession: The Case of Yugoslavia'. *European Journal of International Law* 12, no. 4: 751-779.

Tanzi, Vito and Howell H. Zee. 1998. 'Consequence of the Economic and Monetary Union for the Coordination of Tax Systems in the European Union: Lessons from the US Experience'. IMF Working Paper no. WP/98/115. Washington, DC: IMF.

Tunrovsky, Stephen. 1997. *International Macroeconomic Dynamics*. Cambridge: Massachusetts Institute of Technology Press.

UNIDO. 2003. 'Sudan Industrial Survey'. In *Sudan: The Road Towards Sustainable and Broad –Based Growth*, ed. World Bank. Washington, DC: World Bank.

USAID. 2009. 'South Sudan: Post-Conflict Economic Recovery and Growth: An Agenda for USAID Engagement'. USAID /Sudan Support Project. July.

Van Ham, P. 1994. 'Ukraine, Russia and European Security: Implications for Western Policy'. Chaillot Papers 13. Institute for Security Studies, Western European Union.

Vos, Rob. 2001. 'Currency Volatility and Macroeconomic Policy Coordination in Mercosur'. Paper presented at a Conference on 'Mercosour after 10 years', Leiden University, the Netherlands.

Weeks, John. 2008. 'The Effectiveness of Monetary Policy Reconsidered'. International Poverty Center Technical Paper no. 3, United Nations Development Programme, Brasillia, Brazil.

World Bank. 2008. 'Revitalizing Sudan's Non-Oil Exports: A Diagnostic Trade Integration Study (DTIS)'. Prepared for the Integrated Framework Program, The World Bank Country Office, the Sudan.

—. 2009. 'Sudan: The Road towards Sustainable and Broad-Based Growth'. Poverty Reduction and Economic Management Unit, Africa Region, Washington, DC.

—. (n.d.). *World Development Indicators*. http://data.worldbank.org/indicator.

Young, R. 2002. 'Economic Factors in the Secession Calculus: A Survey'. Paper Presented to the Conference on the Economics of Political Integration and Disintegration. Belgium: Université Catholique de Louvain.

Zahler, Roberrto. 2001. 'Strategies for Monetary Cooperation/Union'. *Integration and Trade* 5, no. 13: 3-34.

# Factors for Successful Performance Management Implementation in a University in Uganda

Bernadette Nambi Karuhanga
Makerere University
and Amanda Werner
Nelson Mandela Metropolitan University

*The purpose of this article is to identify factors that facilitate the successful implementation of institutional performance management at universities in Uganda. A mixed methods approach is employed. Factors for successful performance management implementation were compiled from literature and interviews, which were later developed into a survey instrument that was administered to academic staff in four public universities, selected using a disproportionate stratified random sampling technique. The findings reveal that the factors necessary for successful performance management implementation can be categorised into five principal components, namely: (i) performance framework, performance culture, and employee support; (ii) an individual performance management system; (iii) alignment; (iv) smart goal setting; and (v) tangible and intangible measures. Knowledge of these factors enables managers to ensure that these exist in universities for successful performance management implementation. This article is an empirical contribution to the literature on factors for successful institutional performance management implementation in universities in Uganda.*

## 1. Introduction

There has been an increase in the number of universities in Uganda as a result of the liberalisation of the economy. This increased number has augmented competition with each university, whether private or public, struggling to be the market leader. This has been exacerbated by the unfolding of global markets. Many institutions and organisations are now facing more competitive pressures than at any other point in time. This calls for efficiency, effectiveness, and responsiveness to customer expectations (Halachmi, 2002).

Literature highlights performance management as critical for efficient and effective service delivery (de Waal & Counet, 2009; Neely, 1999). Therefore, any institution aiming at becoming a 'leading edge' organisation should embrace institutional performance management. Universities in Uganda need to successfully implement institutional performance management if they are to favourably compete in the current dynamic environment and become market leaders. The major research question of this article is: how can public universities ensure effective institutional performance management implementation? To answer this question a study was conducted to identify factors required for the successful implementation of institutional performance management at universities in Uganda.

The remainder of this article is organised as follows. We look at the Ugandan context in section 2. We then discuss the benefits of institutional performance management implementation in section 3. We look at the guidelines for the successful implementation of performance management and the research design and methodology of the study in sections 4 and 5, respectively. Finally, we discuss the findings in section 6 and conclude the article in sections 7 and 8.

## 2. Country Context

The liberalisation of the economy of Uganda in the late 1980s and early 1990s opened doors to the private sector to actively participate in the economy (Nakanyike, 2003). This did not only open opportunities for the business sector but the education sector as well. Before liberalisation, the country had only one public university, Makerere University, which has been in existence since 1922. With liberal policies, government funding towards university education was reduced. The largest contribution to university funding now comes from privately sponsored students. The number of universities in the country rose to 34, which comprise 5 public and 29 private universities (New Vision, 2013). This trend has been matched with an increase in student enrolment in universities from approximately 5,000 in 1986 to currently more than 100,000 students in 2011 (Businge, 2011). Among the total student population in the five public universities, only 4,000 students are on government sponsorship in various disciplines every year (Namirembe, 2005).

It is estimated that the government contribution to the funding of public universities as percentage of the Gross Domestic Product averages only 0.3%. This is lower than other countries in East Africa. Resources have not been proportionately increased as compared to the increased student enrolment in most of the universities, which has created a very low student/resources ratio (Businge, 2013). This ratio has, in turn, created major challenges and issues in the management of university education, including congested lecture rooms, food rationing in university kitchens, reduced allowances, low salaries to lecturers, lack of staff development, and failure to expand (Businge, 2013). These seem to compromise the quality of university education. In a study conducted by Karuhanga and Werner (2013) in public universities, it was established that inadequate and limited facilities, limited and uneven cash flows, limited motivation, and low staff morale were among the key challenges impacting institutional performance management implementation.

While there has been an increase in the number of universities in the country, it is estimated that only two out of every 1,000 students are able to enrol for university education. This compares unfavourably to 100 for every 1,000 students in other African countries (Businge, 2013). This implies that universities in the country are still faced with resource constraints. The above challenges require universities to devise ways of ensuring quality service provision, because they have a critical role to play in ensuring that individuals are equipped with higher level skills and are prepared for employment in the competitive market (Nayeri et al, 2008). How then can universities constrained by resources be able to ensure the required quality? It is postulated that the achievement of the above can be facilitated by effective institutional performance management implementation, which has been heralded in the literature as very necessary to both profit and non-profit making institutions.

## 3. Benefits of Institutional Performance Management Implementation

Non-profit making organisations, such as public universities, do not face considerable competition because they have always received protection from the government. This, however, has had a negative impact on their performance (Shun et al, 2006). Clearly, poorly performing organisations cannot survive for long (Flapper et al, 1996). In this regard, institutional performance management is useful to both profit and non-profit organisations. With stiff competition from private higher learning institutions, as a result of the liberalisation of the economy, universities must devise ways of transforming their strategies into activities that will enable them to achieve organisational goals. It is postulated that this can be done by utilising performance management tools (Shun et al, 2006).

The benefits of successful performance management implementation are enormous. Good performance management assures customers of high quality service because each employee will be working effectively towards the achievement of personal and organisational goals (Macaulay & Cook, 1994; Brown, 2005). Furthermore, performance management, as an accountability mechanism, assists managers in the effective management of functional operations and in the decision making process. By embedding performance management in the management systems of an organisation, focus on performance and attainment of strategy will be easily ascertained because it links the strategy, the processes, and the resources to goals (Kaplan & Norton, 1992; Verweire & Berghe, 2003).

The performance management process in itself provides a learning platform for individuals through their involvement in the decision-making process and in the achievement of organisational goals. High performing organisations establish a performance management system as a mechanism to translate vision into performance indicators that are later communicated to all concerned parties (Amaratunga & Baldry, 2002). Hence, it becomes easy to translate the vision into clear outcomes shared by all stakeholders and to determine the extent of organisational success (Amaratunga et al, 2001). The existence of a performance-based management system ensures a systematic method for managing performance objectives, a communication channel to top management and all stakeholders, and the involvement of all concerned in performance improvement and the evaluation process. It also ensures that an accountability framework exists (Artley et al, 2001). It further provides the leadership with a basis for analysing performance results and determining whether there are no unanticipated deviations (Amaratunga & Baldry, 2002).

Brown (2005) provides a number of reasons why organisations introduce performance management, including providing information on the effectiveness and efficiency of employees and the organisation as a whole with the aim of improving performance; directing employees toward priority areas; motivating employees through training and development; creating a basis for rewarding good performance; and providing an accountability framework and a performance oriented culture aimed at customer satisfaction. de Waal, Kourtit, and Nijkamp (2009) have identified a number of advantages of performance management, which they categorised into quantitative and qualitative benefits. The quantitative advantages include increased revenue and profits, reduced costs, and higher return on assets. The qualitative advantages include improved communication and understanding of the organisational strategy, closer coordination and improved knowledge and information sharing among organisational units, and a better focus on the vital organisational issues. Other advantages include increased focus on the achievement of goals, better quality of performance information, strategic alignment of organisational units, increased operational efficiency, better management quality, and an improved decision-making process.

Empirical studies show that performance management has enabled organisations to improve their performance. In a study carried out by Brown (2005) in primary schools in England, participants agreed that the implementation of performance management under favourable conditions enhances quality. The introduction of the performance management system by the Botswana National Productivity Centre (BNPC) in the public service in Botswana yielded positive results. Strategic plans, which never existed prior to the implementation of the performance management system, were developed. A working document that guided the implementation of the mandates of government ministries was designed and a Performance Management Manual was developed. This provided guidance in the development of the professional management system and the promotion of civil society evaluation of the performance of government ministries (Dzimbiri, 2008).

Ofori and Atiogbe (2011) conducted a study in universities in Ghana. They established that monitoring, evaluation, and control facilitated the decision-making process as managers were able to keep track of the programmes with the anticipated performance targets. In a study conducted by de Waal (2007) in a college of business in Tanzania, it was documented that efforts made by the management of the college to improve performance included adopting a performance management system through the application of the Performance Management Analysis (PMA) radar diagram. Therefore, it would be prudent for all strategic organisations, whether public or private, to focus on implementing effective performance management systems. It is through such systems that they can remain highly competitive (Artley et al, 2001).

There has been no study that has been conducted in Uganda to identify the factors relevant for successful institutional performance management implementation. Public universities in the country are not profit oriented. They, however, continue to receive insufficient budget allocations. Furthermore, the university fees paid by students on private sponsorship are below cost. The United Nations Development Programme (UNDP) estimates the annual cost of university education in Africa at between US$10,000 – US$15,000 per programme (Businge, 2013). Yet students on private sponsorship only pay on average US$1,200 per annum per programme. Universities are therefore faced with severe resource constraints. With such resource constraints, the implementation of the institutional performance management system is crucial. However, universities in Uganda, a developing country, must be mindful of their context (Mendonca & Kanungo, 1996) while implementing the institutional performance management system.

## 4. Guidelines for Successful Institutional Performance Management Implementation

Performance information is as good as useless if it is not used for the intended purpose (de Waal, 2004). The implementation of performance management is vital to the realisation of organisational goals (de Waal, 2003). Existing literature reveals a number of guidelines for the successful implementation of performance management. These have been compiled and summarised in table 1 below.

de Waal (2004) developed a performance management analysis (PMA) radar for use by organisations to determine the extent to which they implement performance management. The PMA portrays structural and behavioural factors required in performance management implementation. The structural side of the PMA focuses on the required system that must be in place for successful performance management implementation. The behavioural side focuses on the extent to which employees use the performance management system (de Waal & Gerristen, 2006). The PMA emphasises that the two areas require equal attention. Table 2 presents the factors de Waal (2004) identified for the successful implementation of performance management.

**Table 1: Guidelines for the successful implementation of performance management**

| Factor | Definition | Source |
|---|---|---|
| Objectives | Focus on key but limited objectives due to resource constraints. The goals should be clear. The objectives should be specific, measurable, achievable, realistic, and challenging. | Kaplan, 2001, 359; Ball & Halwachi, 1987, 397; Otley, 1999, 365; Halachmi, 2002, 65; Brown, 2005, 481. |
| Customer focus | Customer focus should be on meeting customer expectations. | Verweire & van den Berghe, 2003, 784. |
| Leadership commitment | Leadership should be fully committed and involved in the entire performance management process. | Verweire & van den Berghe, 2003, 784; Bourne et al, 2000, 761; Halachmi, 2002, 65; Ingram, 1997, 297. |
| Management style | Management style should promote manager-subordinate relationship. | Mendonca & Kanungo, 1996, 74. |
| Efficient and effective information/ communication system | There should be timely and clear communication not only internally, top-down and bottom-up within the entire organisation, but also externally. | Verweire & van den Berghe, 2003, 784; Amaratunga & Baldry, 2002, 221; Otley, 1999, 365; Bourne et al, 2000, 762; Kagaari et al, 2010. |
| Strategic alignment | Individual activities and all other functions of the organisation should be aligned to the strategic goals | Verweire & van den Berghe, 2003, 784; Halachmi, 2002, 65. |
| Conceptual framework | A framework for managing the implementation process must be in place. | Artley et al, 2001, 3. |
| A reward system | A system should be in place to reward good performance; poor performance should be encouraged and motivated to improve because the performance management system is not a punishment tool but an improvement tool. | Artley & Stroh, 2001, 3; Amaratunga & Baldry, 2002, 221; Otley, 1999, 365; Werveire & van den Berghe, 2003, 783; Ohemeng, 2009, 112; Halachmi, 2002, 65. |

| | | |
|---|---|---|
| Shared understanding of mission, vision, and strategies, and continuous learning and training | Should aim at creating awareness and promoting learning and a shared understanding of the vision, mission, values, strategic direction, key performance measures, meaning of performance management, and its usefulness to the institution. | Otley, 1999, 365; Ohemeng, 2009, 112; Brown, 2005, 481; Ohemeng, 2009, 112; Amaratunga & Baldry, 2002, 221. |
| Performance standards | Should be set collectively. | Verweire & van den Berghe, 2003, 783 |
| Review process & planning | There is need to continuously review the process. | Ohemeng, 2009, 112 |
| Performance oriented culture | Develop a culture which promotes individual accountability, teamwork, and responsibility. | Castka et al, 2001, 123; Ingram, 1997, 300; Chau, 2008, 116; Brown, 2005, 481; Halachmi, 2002, 65; de Waal, 2004, 308. |
| Intangible measures and Key Performance Indicators (KPIs) | Identify the intangible measures of performance to supplement the financial measures and the KPIs. | Amaratunga et al, 2001, 180; Brown, 2005, 481; Kaplan & Norton, 2000. |
| Employee commitment and buy in | A committed and supportive workforce is necessary for implementation. | Bourne et al, 2000, 761; Halchmi, 2002, 65. |
| Maturity alignment | Consideration of all components of the stage of development at which the organisation is, is vital in performance management. | Verweire & van den Berghe, 2003, 782, 784. |
| Effective budget | Set priorities and adhere to the budget. | Halachmi, 2002, 65. |
| Clear roles and responsibility | Individual roles & responsibilities should be clear. | Halachmi, 2002, 65 |
| Cultural factors | The culture should be aligned with the vision and strategic direction. | Mendonca & Kanungo, 1996, 68-69. |

**Table 2: The nine-dimensions of the performance management analysis**

| Dimension | Side | Description |
|---|---|---|
| Responsibility culture | Structural | A clear parenting style and tasks and responsibilities have been defined and these are applied consistently at all management levels. |
| Content | Structural | Organisational members use a set of financial and non-financial performance information, which has a strategic focus through the use of KCFs (write in full) and KPIs. |
| Integrity | Structural | The performance information is reliable, timely and consistent. |
| Manageability | Structural | Management reports and performance management systems are user-friendly and more detailed performance information is easily accessible through information communication technology (ICT) systems. |
| Accountability | Behavioural | Organisational members feel responsible for the results of the KPIs of both their own responsibility areas and the organisation as a whole. |
| Management style | Behavioural | Senior management is visibly interested and involved in the performance of organisational members and stimulates an improvement culture and proactive behaviour. At the same time, it consistently confronts organisational members with lagging results. |
| Action orientation | Behavioural | Performance information is integrated in the daily activities of organisational members in such a way that problems are immediately addressed and (corrective or preventive) actions taken |

| | | |
|---|---|---|
| Communication | Behavioural | Communication about the results (top-down and bottom-up) takes place at regular intervals as well as the sharing of knowledge and performance information between organisational units. |
| Alignment | Behavioural | Other management systems in the organisation, such as the human resource management system, are aligned with performance management, so what is important to the organisation is regularly evaluated and rewarded. |

Source: Adapted from de Waal, 2004, 308

de Waal (2003) suggested that there was need to carry out further studies to explore additional behavioural, environmental, or organisational factors required for the successful implementation of a performance management system. It was, therefore, necessary to identify additional factors from the literature that may facilitate effective performance management implementation, other than those mentioned above by de Waal (2004). The above factors were captured in the survey instrument, which was used to confirm perceived factors required for the successful implementation of institutional performance management at public universities in Uganda.

## 5. Research Design and Methodology

The study adopted a cross-sectional survey design with a mixed methods approach. Factors for successful performance management implementation were compiled from the literature. The findings were developed into a survey instrument that was later administered to 350 respondents in four public universities in Uganda. The survey instrument consisted of a questionnaire made of 20 closed and 1 open ended question. The choice of this instrument was based on the fact that questionnaires could be completed by respondents at their convenience since the period in which data was collected was a busy period for universities. During the survey, individuals were asked to provide information regarding the extent to which they agreed that the listed factors in the survey were necessary for successful performance management implementation in universities in Uganda. A five item Likert scale was used, ranging from strongly agree (5) to strongly disagree (1). Likert scales were used because they provide a uniform measure and allow for a wider coverage in terms of sample size

(Sarantakos, 1998). The open ended question allowed respondents to provide any additional factors they considered not to have been revealed by the close ended questions. Data were first sorted, coded, and then entered in the SPSS version 17 programme for analysis.

## Study Population and Sampling Technique

The population size of the four universities was 2,231 (.2231). According to Krejcie and Morgan's (1970) model, the appropriate sample size for a population ranging from 2,200 to 2,400 should not exceed 331 respondents. Out of the 350 questionnaires distributed to respondents, 330 fully answered questionnaires were considered for this study (Sekaran, 2003).

The target population for the survey included academic staff from four out of the five public universities in Uganda. These are Makerere University (MAK), Kyambogo University (KYU), Mbarara University of Science and Technology (MUST), and Gulu University. Respondents were selected using a disproportionate stratified random sampling technique with the faculties/schools/institutes forming the strata. This is because faculties/schools/institutes did not have the same number of academic staff yet it was necessary to have each stratum represented.

## Data Analysis and Ethical Considerations

Qualitative and quantitative methods were both used to analyse data. The closed questions of the questionnaire were subjected to statistical methods of analysis, while the responses from the open ended question was qualitatively analysed. Mean scores and standard deviations were calculated to obtain the measures of central tendency of deviation. The Cronbach's alpha was used to measure internal consistency and reliability. A Cronbach's value ranging from 0.70 was considered appropriate for measuring internal consistency (Sekaran, 2003). Correlations between demographic and non-demographical variables were made. Principal component analysis extraction method was used to reduce the items to a smaller number without necessarily losing meaning. The varimax rotation with Keizer normalization method, eigenvalues greater than one and the scree plot criteria were used. The Kaiser-Meyer-Olkin (KMO) test and Bartlett's test for sphericity were conducted to determine if the items could be factored.

Content analysis was utilised to analyse the open ended question. Content analysis has been appraised as a powerful tool for data reduction (Stemler, 2001). Emergent coding was applied to the data collected and data was later classified based on the themes that were developed (Stemler, 2001). Content analysis is used to code open ended questions in a survey (Weber, 1990). The frequency of responses in respect of each developed theme was determined. We revisited the responses to establish the context in which the statements were made with an aim of strengthening the validity of the findings.

A pilot study was conducted in one of the four public universities to check on ambiguities in the data collection instrument (Yin, 2003) and to ensure that only relevant and correct questions were asked (Sarantakos, 1998; Sekaran, 2003). All ambiguities were cleared during the final study. The findings and proposals from the pilot study were taken into consideration during the final questionnaire development.

We sought permission from the relevant authorities to conduct the research at the four public universities. We also sought the consent of the respondents. Only willing respondents participated in the study (Chava & Nachmias, 2003). The anonymity of the respondents was guaranteed and information provided was treated with utmost confidentiality (Sarantakos, 1988; Chava & Nachmias, 2003; Sekaran, 2003).

## 6. Findings

The developed survey instrument was used to confirm perceived factors required for the successful implementation of institutional performance management at public universities in Uganda. The first part of the study required respondents to provide information relating to demographic data, such as the university they worked for, years in employment, the nature of appointment, the highest level of education, the gender, and the level of responsibility. The number of respondents was proportionate to the population size of each university represented in the sample. Thus, 66.4% came from Makerere University, 18.2% from Kyambogo University, 6.7% from Mbarara University of Science and Technology, and 8.8% from Gulu University.

The study revealed that 16.1% of the respondents had been working for their respective university for less than 3 years, 21.8% for 3 to 5 years, 27.6% for 6 to 10 years, 14.5% for 11 to 15 years, 10.9% for 16 to 20 years, and 9.1% for more than 20 years. Overall, 83.9% of the respondents had been employed at their respective universities for a period of three or more years. A total of 62.1% had been employed for longer than five years.

Seventeen% of the respondents were part time, while 83% were full time staff. Taking into consideration the time most staff have spent at their respective universities, and the number of full time staff who participated in the study, it could be postulated that the majority of staff were acquainted with the performance management systems in their respective universities. They could, therefore, advise on what they consider vital for successful institutional performance management implementation.

In terms of education, 10.3% of the respondents had a Bachelor's degree as their highest level of education, 60.9% had a Master's degree, and 27.3% had a Doctor of Philosophy degree. Only 1.5% of the respondents had other qualifications. The results indicate that the majority of the members of staff at the various universities had a Master's degree. This is estimated at 60.9%. Of these only 26.7% were female, while 73.3% were male.

The level of staff responsibility was also examined. The survey showed that 17% of the respondents were at a senior management level, and 40% were at were at a middle management level. A further 43% were employed at non-supervisory level, with a relatively large group falling in the categories of senior and middle management levels. This was estimated at 57%. It was postulated that the responses of this study provide a true and fair picture of factors for successful performance management implementation at the various units in public universities in Uganda since the majority of the respondents held a management position in a university.

The second part of the study required respondents to indicate the extent to which they agreed that the factors indicated in the questionnaire are necessary for performance management implementation in the universities in which they worked. In order to measure the internal consistency and reliability of the items measuring the 'factors required for successful performance management implementation' construct, a Cronbach's alpha test was done, revealing an alpha of .907.

An analysis of the mean scores of the items in the questionnaire revealed an aggregate mean score of 4.34. This showed a tendency in the responses to mostly agree and strongly agree. Item 3 (mainly focusing on customer expectations) obtained the lowest mean score of 3.74 and the highest standard deviation of 1.068. The rest of the items obtained a mean score of more than 4.00. Several items such as 2 (Formulation of SMART objectives), 6 (Leadership commitment), 13 (Teamwork), 20 (Employee support), 12 (Clear roles and responsibilities), and 7 (A supportive management style) obtained mean scores of 4.5 and above. This indicated strong agreement among respondents that the formulation of SMART objectives, leadership commitment, teamwork, employee support, clear roles and responsibilities, and a supportive management style were perceived as major factors for the successful implementation of institutional performance management at public universities in the country. Item 2 (Formulation of SMART goals) had the lowest standard deviation of .662; hence, there was agreement among respondents with regard to this item.

The results from the study revealed that the mean scores on the items in table 3 below showed a tendency towards agree responses. This implies that respondents agreed that the following factors were necessary for successful performance management implementation at universities in the country.

**Table 3: Factors necessary for successful performance management implementation**

| Number | Item Factor | Mean Score |
|---|---|---|
| 1 | Focus on a limited number of key objectives | 4.06 |
| 3 | Focus on customer expectations | 3.74 |
| 4 | A reward system linked to performance | 4.3 |
| 5 | Availability of collectively set performance standards | 4.31 |
| 8 | Aligning individual activities with organisation objectives | 4.19 |
| 9 | Aligning all organisational functions to strategic goals | 4.25 |
| 10 | Tangible and intangible measures | 4.36 |
| 11 | Key performance indicators | 4.41 |
| 14 | Mutual respect | 4.4 |
| 15 | An adequate ICT system | 4.4 |
| 16 | A framework to manage the implementation process | 4.29 |
| 17 | Shared understanding of mission, vision, and strategies | 4.4 |
| 18 | Continuous training and learning | 4.44 |
| 19 | A performance oriented culture | 4.41 |

Public universities in the country must, therefore, ensure that the factors in table 3 are in existence for the successful implementation of institutional performance management. A standard deviation ranging from .662 (item 2 - Formulation of SMART objectives) to 1.068 (item 3 - mainly focusing on customer expectations) indicated agreement among respondents with regard to factors for the successful implementation of institutional performance management at public universities in Uganda.

The corrected item total correlation and the Cronbach's alpha, if item is deleted, were done. The results revealed that item 1 (focus on a limited number of objectives) showed the lowest correlation with the rest of the items (.183), raising the Cronbach's alpha to .913, if it is deleted. This was followed by item 2 (mainly focus on customer expectations) with a correlation of .284, increasing the Cronbach's alpha to .912, if it is deleted. The increase in the Cronbach's alpha is negligible as it would remain the same if rounded off to one decimal position. In addition, items 1 and 2 had a high mean score. These items were, therefore, retained.

In order to reduce the number of variables, while maintaining the underlying items, a Principal Component Analysis (PCA) was done. A Kaiser-Meyer-Olkin (KOM) test and the Bartlett's test of sphericity revealed a value of .920. This is considered adequate for factor analysis because it indicates that the items had a compact pattern of correlations (Shu & Chuang, 2011). Bartlett's test was significant ($p < 0.05$) for all scales. Hence, the correlation matrix is not an identity matrix. It was, therefore, possible to conduct a factor analysis (Shu & Chuang, 2011; Field, 2005).

## Principal Component Analysis

Four principal components that had an eigenvalue of greater than 1.00 with the respective items loading to each factor were revealed after applying the eigenvalue-one criterion and a scree plot. All factor loadings less than 0.5 were excluded for easy interpretation of the results.

**Table 4: Total variance explained**

| Component | Initial Eigenvalues | | | Extraction Sums of Squared Loadings | | | Rotation Sums of Squared Loadings | | |
|---|---|---|---|---|---|---|---|---|---|
| | Total | % of Variance | Cumulative% | Total | % of Variance | Cumulative% | Total | % of Variance | Cumulative% |
| 1 | 7.870 | 39.352 | 39.352 | 7.870 | 39.352 | 39.352 | 4.314 | 21.569 | 21.569 |
| 2 | 1.309 | 6.547 | 45.899 | 1.309 | 6.547 | 45.899 | 4.028 | 20.140 | 41.709 |
| 3 | 1.200 | 6.000 | 51.898 | 1.200 | 6.000 | 51.898 | 1.562 | 7.812 | 49.521 |
| 4 | 1.067 | 5.334 | 57.232 | 1.067 | 5.334 | 57.232 | 1.542 | 7.712 | 57.232 |
| 5 | .957 | 4.785 | 62.018 | | | | | | |
| 6 | .884 | 4.418 | 66.435 | | | | | | |
| 7 | .764 | 3.819 | 70.255 | | | | | | |
| 8 | .738 | 3.690 | 73.945 | | | | | | |
| 9 | .679 | 3.393 | 77.338 | | | | | | |
| 10 | .601 | 3.005 | 80.343 | | | | | | |
| 11 | .573 | 2.864 | 83.207 | | | | | | |
| 12 | .509 | 2.546 | 85.753 | | | | | | |
| 13 | .486 | 2.429 | 88.183 | | | | | | |
| 14 | .425 | 2.124 | 90.306 | | | | | | |
| 15 | .384 | 1.920 | 92.227 | | | | | | |
| 16 | .360 | 1.801 | 94.027 | | | | | | |
| 17 | .351 | 1.757 | 95.784 | | | | | | |
| 18 | .316 | 1.578 | 97.362 | | | | | | |
| 19 | .278 | 1.389 | 98.751 | | | | | | |
| 20 | .250 | 1.249 | 100.000 | | | | | | |

It is evident from Table 4 above that the four principal components accounted for 57.23% of the total cumulative variance. Before rotation, component 1 accounted for 39.352%, compared to less than 10% for each of the other components. However, after extraction, component 1 accounted for only 21.569% of the variance compared to 20.140%, 7.812%, and 7.712%, respectively.

**Table 5: Showing a summary of the four principal components with their item loadings and alpha**

| *(i) Component one: performance framework, performance culture, and employee support* | | | |
|---|---|---|---|
| Item | Description | Loadings | Alpha |
| 14 | Mutual respect | .629 | .865 |
| 15 | An adequate ICT system | .616 | |
| 16 | A framework to manage the implementation process | .690 | |
| 17 | Shared understanding of mission, vision and strategies | .730 | |
| 18 | continuous training and learning | .727 | |
| 19 | A performance oriented culture | .651 | |
| 20 | Employee support | .672 | |
| *(ii) Component two: An individual performance management system* | | | |
| 4 | A reward system linked to performance | .706 | .866 |
| 5 | Availability of Collectively set performance standards | .740 | |
| 6 | Leadership commitment | .747 | |
| 7 | Supportive management style | .633 | |
| 11 | Key performance indicators | .550 | |
| 12 | Clear roles and responsibilities | .643 | |
| 13 | Teamwork | .562 | |
| *(iii) Component three: alignment* | | | |
| 8 | Aligning individual activities with organisation objectives | .501 | .69 |
| 9 | Aligning all organisational functions to strategic goals | .561 | |
| *(iv) Component four: Smart goal setting* | | | |
| 1 | Focus on a limited number of key objectives | .736 | .38 |
| 2 | Formulation of SMART objectives | .634 | |

Item 10 (Tangible and intangible measures) did not load on to any component. This implies that this particular item did not correlate with any of the principal components. It was noted that this item had a high mean score (4.36) with a standard deviation of .715. This implies agreement among respondents that this particular factor is necessary for successful institutional performance management implementation. It was, therefore, not deleted.

Three items previously loaded to component 3. These are items 3, 8, and 9. The reliability test results revealed a Cronbach's alpha of .55 for principal component 3. This alpha was below the recommended alpha. Therefore, item 3 was deleted based on the fact that it had the lowest mean score and the highest standard deviation. After deleting item 3, the Cronbach's alpha increased to .69.

The alpha for the items that loaded to component 4 was very low. Hence, there was no implied internal consistency or reliability among the items of component 4. Despite the above, the mean score of these two items was above average (item 1 – 4.06; item 2 – 4.52), with responses tending towards 'strongly agree'. If item 1 is deleted, the overall alpha increases to .913, and if item 2 is deleted the overall alpha is reduced to .905. But since the mean scores for the two items are high and change in the alpha was negligible if the items were deleted, items 1 and 2 were not deleted from the list.

The factors that are required for successful performance management implementation could be categorised into five principal components. These are: (i) performance framework, performance culture, and employee support; (ii) an individual performance management system; (iii) alignment; (iv) smart goal setting; and (v) availability of tangible and intangible measures. This is based on the results from the analysis of the close ended questions.

A Pearson correlation conducted on the data revealed that the correlation coefficients between items were all below 0.9. No item had a majority of significance values greater than 0.05. Hence, there was no need to delete any item at this point. Field (2005) advises that if an item has a coefficient greater than 0.9 with majority of the significance values greater than 0.05, then there are dangers of singularity in the data.

## Qualitative Analysis

Respondents were also requested to indicate any other factors they perceived as necessary for successful performance management implementation at public universities. Sixteen% of the respondents indicated various factors that they felt were relevant for performance management implementation in public universities in the country. The total number of responses per factor was counted to determine the number of times they occurred. The other factors most indicated vital for successful performance management implementation by most of the respondents are shown in table 6.

**Table 6: Showing other factors considered relevant for successful performance management implementation**

| Theme | Frequency |
|---|---|
| Motivation of employees | 25 |
| All inclusive decision making | 18 |
| Effective communication | 10 |
| Training and awareness | 10 |
| Adequate funding | 10 |
| Effective feedback | 7 |

However, among the other factors indicated by respondents, those that were not traced from the literature review and had not been mentioned in the survey instrument were: *adequate funding, an effective feedback process, openness and transparency, a conducive study/working environment, effective evaluation system, autonomy of the university, collective responsibility, flexibility, individual responsibility, low lecturer students' ratio, decentralisation of power, and functional quality assurance.*

## 7. Discussion of Results and Conclusion

The purpose of the study was to determine the factors necessary for the successful institutional performance management implementation in public universities in Uganda. Universities must ensure that implementation of this strategy is successful to have an advantage in the current competitive and dynamic environment by ensuring that the factors that facilitate successful institutional performance management implementation are in place and taken into consideration.

Four principal components were extracted under which the necessary factors for institutional performance management implementation were categorised. These are (i) performance framework, performance culture, and employee support; (ii) an individual performance management system; (iii) alignment; and (iv) smart goal setting. An additional factor was taken into consideration, (v) availability of tangible and intangible measures, because of a high mean score (4.36) with a standard deviation of .715, which implies agreement among respondents that this particular factor is necessary for institutional performance management implementation. The qualitative analysis revealed that motivation of employees, all inclusive decision making, effective communication, training and awareness, adequate funding, and effective feedback were perceived as vital for successful performance management implementation by majority of the respondents.

A framework for managing the implementation process (Artley & Stroh, 2001), continuous training and learning about performance management implementation (Amaratunga & Baldry, 2002), and existence of a performance oriented culture (Brown, 2005, 481) facilitate performance management implementation. But, most importantly, successful performance management implementation requires full commitment and involvement of both management and employees (Kaplan, 2001; Amaratunga & Baldry, 2002; Shun et al, 2006; Sole, 2009). An efficient and effective ICT system plays a vital role in the communication and data collection processes (Bourne et al, 2000), and horizontal and vertical communication is necessary (Amaratunga & Baldry, 2002), as it promotes shared understanding of events in the entire institution and clarifies expectations of individuals at each point in time.

Several factors have been supported by the literature as vital for successful performance management implementation. Among these are the existence of a reward system linked to performance (Otley, 1999; Artley & Stroh, 2001; Amaratunga & Baldry, 2002; Shun et al, 2006); availability of collectively set performance standards; leadership commitment (Halachmi, 2002; Verweire & van den Bergh, 2003); a supportive management style (Mendonca & Kanungo, 1996); identification of key performance indicators (de Waal, 2004); giving clear roles and responsibilities to employees (Halachmi, 2002); and teamwork. Teams create synergies (Ingram, 1997; Castka et al, 2001), which result in excellent performance. When individuals work in a team, coordination and communication become easy and individual creativity is enhanced. Further, teamwork promotes cohesion within an organisation. It develops individuals' sense of belonging and promotes commitment and motivation among the team members (Ingram, 1997). Committed employees will do what it takes for the sake of the organisation. Therefore, public universities in Uganda must work towards the enhancement of teamwork for the successful implementation of the performance management system.

Component 3 was labelled 'alignment' with two items loading to it: aligning individual activities with organisation objectives and aligning all organisational functions to strategic objectives. There must be a link between the strategies and the process of goal setting, operational support, control, and organisational behaviour processes (Verweire & van den Bergh, 2003). The alignment of compensation with organisation strategies is also vital (Verweire & van den Bergh, 2003) for successful performance management implementation.

Component 4, labelled 'SMART goal setting', had two items loading on it: a focus on a limited number of key objectives and formulation of SMART objectives. Ball and Halwachi (1987) and Kaplan (2001) note that developing countries face a constraint in terms of limited resources. Much as a government might be mandated to finance its public universities, a developing country faces financial constraints. This has resulted into decreasing government budget allocations to public universities (Businge, 2013). This has been further exacerbated by the limited contribution from privately sponsored students to university education. Hence, universities in Uganda must have limited objectives that can be achieved within the limits of the available resources.

In summary, all the factors indicated, except item 10 (tangible and intangible measures), loaded to a component. Item 10 had a high mean score and low standard deviation. It was, therefore, retained. Item 3 loaded to component three but was later deleted because the alpha was low. The alpha increased when the item was deleted. Since the item had the lowest mean score and highest standard deviation, it was excluded. The remaining 19 items were considered necessary for the successful implementation of institutional performance management. The results from the study are therefore congruent with the variables considered in the theoretical study.

## 8. Policy Implications and Study Limitations

Knowledge of the factors for performance management implementation enables managers to ensure that these exist in universities for successful performance management implementation. Management should strive for an effective performance management framework and culture. These should be focused on individual accountability, teamwork, and responsibility. The organisational goals should be in alignment with the college/faculty/schools/departmental /individual goals to ensure successful implementation. Tangible and intangible indicators must be identified to facilitate measurement of performance. Universities must ensure that the implementation of the strategy is successful if they are to maintain a leading edge in the current competitive and dynamic environment. This study, therefore, provides a number of factors that universities in Uganda must ensure that they are in existence for the successful institutional performance management implementation and to which attention must be paid.

In the study we looked at only four public universities in Uganda. The results of this study might, therefore, not be conclusive in giving a general picture in all universities in Uganda. Secondly not all factors may have been captured from literature to warrant the above indicated factors as conclusive. In addition, factors impacting performance management implementation in Uganda may not necessarily be applicable to all institutions of higher learning and in all developing countries. Further research is, therefore, required to confirm the factors for successful performance management implementation in all universities in Uganda. A comparative study could be conducted to establish if there exists any difference in perceptions regarding factors for successful performance management implementation between public and private universities. Despite the above limitations, it is hoped that the results of this study will ignite further research interests in performance management implementation in institutions of higher learning in the developing world.

## References

Amaratunga, D., D. Baldry, and S. Marjan. 2001. 'Process Improvement through Performance Measurement: The Balanced Scorecard Methodology'. *Work Study* 50, no. 5: 179-188.

Amaratunga, D. and D. Baldry. 2002. 'Moving from Performance Measurement to Performance Management'. *Emerald* 20, no. 5-6: 217-223.

Amaratunga, D. and D. Baldry. 2003. 'A Conceptual Framework to Measure Facilities Management Performance'. *Property Management* 21, no. 2: 171-189.

Artley, W. and S. Stroh. 2001. 'The Performance-based Management Handbook: Establishing an Integrated Performance Measurement System'. http://www.orau.gov/pbm.

Artley, W., D. J. Ellison, and B. Kennedy. 2001. *The Performance-based Management Handbook: A six-volume Compilation of Techniques and Tools for Implementing the Government Performance and Results Act of 1993*. Oak Ridge, TN: Performance-based Management Special Interest Group.

Ball, R. and J. Halwachi. 1987. 'Performance Indicators in Higher Education'. *Higher Education* 16, no. 4: 393-405.

Bititci, U., A. Carrie, and L. McDevitt. 1997. 'Integrated Performance Measurement Systems: An Audit and Development Guide'. *The TQM Magazine* 9, no. 1.

Bourne, M., J. Mills, M. Wilcox, A. Neely, and K. Platts. 2000. 'Designing, Implementing and Updating Performance Measurement Systems'. *International Journal of Operations and Production Management* 20, no. 7: 754-771.

Brown, A. 2005. 'Implementing Performance Management in England's Primary Schools'. *International Journal of Productivity and Performance Management* 54, no. 5-6: 468- 481.

Businge, C. 2011. '70,000 to Miss Admission to University'. *New Vision*. http://www.Sundayvision.co.ug/.

—. 2013. 'Higher Education in Uganda'. *New Vision*. http://www.sundayvision.co.ug/.

Castka, P., C. J. Bamber, J. M. Sharp, and P. Belohoubek. 2001. 'Factors Affecting Successful Implementation of High Performance Teams'. *Team Performance Management: An International Journal* 7, no. 7-8: 123-134.

Chau, S. V. 2008. 'The Relationship of Strategic Performance Management to Team Strategy, Company Performance and Organisational Effectiveness'. *Team Performance Management* 14, no. 3-4: 113-117.

Chava, F. N. and D. Nachmias. 2003. *Research Methods in the Social Sciences*. Fifth edition. London: Replika Press.

Dandira. M. 2011. 'Involvement of Implementers: Missing Element in Strategy Formulation'. *Business Strategy Series* 12, no. 1: 30-34.

de Waal, A. A. 2003. 'Behavioural Factors Important for the Successful Implementation and Use of Performance Management Systems'. *Management Decision* 41, no. 8: 688-697.

—. 2004. 'Stimulating Performance-driven Behaviour to Obtain Better Results'. *International Journal of Productivity and Performance Management* 53, no. 4: 301 – 316.

de Waal. A. A. and G. Gerritsen-Medema. 2006. 'Performance Management Analysis: A Case Study at a Dutch Municipality'. *International Journal of Productivity and Performance Management* 55, no. 1: 26-39.

de Waal, A. A. 2007. 'Is Performance Management Applicable in Developing Countries? The Case of a Tanzanian College'. *International Journal of Emerging Markets* 2, no. 1: 69-83.

de Waal, A. A. and H. Counet. 2009. 'Lessons Learned from Performance Management Systems Implementations'. *International Journal of Productivity and Performance Management* 58, no. 4: 367-390.

de Waal, A. A., K. Kourtit, and P. Nijkamp. 2009. 'The Relationship between the Level of Completeness of a Strategic Performance Management System and Perceived Advantages and Disadvantages'. *International Journal of Operations and Production Management* 25, no. 12: 1242-1265.

Dzimbiri, L. B. 2008. 'Experiences in New Public Management in Africa: The Case of Performance Management Systems in Botswana'. *African Development* 33, no. 4: 43-58.

Druckman, D., J. E. Singer, and H. V. Cott. 1997. 'Enhancing Organisational Performance: Organisational Culture'. *National Academy of Sciences* http://www.nap.edu.

Elzinga, T., B. Albronda, and F. Kluijtmans. 2009. 'Behavioural Factors Influencing Performance Management Systems' Use'. *International Journal of Productivity and Performance Management* 58, no. 6: 508-522.

Eupal, F. 2009. 'Uganda Higher Education Inferior'. *The Observer*. http://www.observer.ug.

Field, A. P. 2005. *Discovering Statistics using SPSS*. Second edition. London: Sage.

Flapper, P. D. S., L. Fortuin, and P. P. M. Stoop. 1996. 'Towards Consistent Performance Management Systems'. *International Journal of Operations and Production Management* 16, no. 7: 27-37.

Halachmi, A. 2002. 'Performance Measurement and Government Productivity'. *Work Study* 51, no. 2: 63 -73.

Handler, A., M. Issel, and B. Turnock. 2001. 'A Conceptual Framework to Measure Performance of the Public Health System'. *American Journal of Public Health* 91, no. 8: 1235-1239.

Ingram, H. 1997. 'Performance Management: Processes, Quality and Team Working'. *International Journal of Contemporary Hospitality Management* 9, no. 7: 295-303.

Kagaari, J. R. K., C. J. Munene, and M. J. Ntayi. 2010. 'Performance Management Practices: Information and Communication Technology (ICT) Adoption and Managed Performance'. *Quality Assurance in Education* 18, no. 2: 106-125.

Kaplan, R. S. and D. P. Norton. 1992. 'The Balanced Score Card: Measures that Drive Performance'. *Harvard Business Review* 70, no. 1: 71-79.

Kaplan, R. S. and D. P. Norton. 2000. 'Using the Balanced Score Card as a Strategic Management System'. *Harvard Business Review* 4126.

Kaplan, R. S. 2001. 'Strategic Performance Measurement and Management in Non Profit Organisations'. *Nonprofit Management & Leadership* 11, no. 3: 353-370.

Karen, F., A. Jiju, S. and Ogden. 2009. 'Performance Management in the Public Sector'. *International Journal of Public Sector Management* 22, no. 6: 478-498.

Karuhanga, B. N. and A. Werner. 2013. 'Challenges Impacting Performance Management Implementation in Public Universities: A Case of Uganda'. *African Journal of Economic and Management Studies* 4, no. 2: 223-243

Kloot, L. and J. Martin. 2000. 'Strategic Performance Management: A Balanced Approach to Performance Management Issues in Local Government'. *Management Accounting Research*11: 231-251.

Krejcie, R. and D. Morgan. 1970. 'Determining Sample Size for Research Activities'. *Educational and Psychological Measurement* 30: 607-610.

Macaulay, S. and S. Cook. 1994. 'Performance Management as the Key to Customer Service'. *Industrial and Commercial Training* 26, no. 11: 3-8.

Marcoulides, G. A. and H. R. Heck. 1993. 'Organisational Culture and Performance: Proposing and Testing a Model'. *Organisational Science* 4, no. 2: 209-225.

Mendonca, M. and R. N. Kanungo. 1996. 'Impact of Culture on Performance Management in Developing Countries'. *International Journal of Manpower* 17, no. 4-5: 65-75.

Nakanyike, B. M. 2003. 'Country Higher Education Profiles'. www.bc.edu/bcorg/avp/soe/cihe/inhea/profiles/Uganda.htm.

Namirembe, G. B. 2005. *Ministerial Seminar on Education for Rural People in Africa: Status of Education for Rural People. Policy Lessons, Options and Priorities.* Country report: Uganda. Addis Ababa, Ethiopia, 7-9 September.

Nayeri, M. D., M. M. Mashhadi, K. Mohajeri. 2008. 'Universities Strategic Evaluation Using Balanced Score Card'. *Proceedings of World Academy of Science, Engineering and Technology* 27: 332-337.

Neely, A. D. 1999. 'The Performance Measurement Revolution: Why Now and What Next'. *International Journal of Operations and Production Management* 19, no. 2: 205-228.

Ofori, D. and E. Atiogbe. 2011. 'Strategic Planning in Public Universities: A Developing Country Perspective'. *Business and Management Review* 1, no. 7: 68-85.

Ohemeng, F. L. K. 2009. 'Constraints in the Implementation of Performance Management Systems in Developing Countries. The Ghanaian Case'. *International Journal of Cross Cultural Management* 9, no. 1:109-132.

Otley, D. 1999. 'Performance Management: A Framework for Management Control Systems Research'. *Management Accounting Research* 10, no. 4: 363-382.

Raduan, C. R., N. Kumar, H. Abdullah, and G. Y. Ling. 2008. 'Organisational Culture as a Root of Performance Improvement: Research Recommendations'. *Contemporary Management Research* 4, no. 1: 43-56.

Rashid, Z. A., M. Sambasivan, and J. Johari. 2003. 'The Influence of Corporate Culture and Organisational Commitment on Performance'. *Journal of Management Development* 22, no. 8: 708-728.

Sarantakos, S. 1998. *Social Research.* South Melbourne, Australia: Palgrave. Macmillan Publishers Ltd.

Sekaran, U. 2003. 'Research Methods for Business. A Skill Building Approach'. New York: Wiley.

Shu, W. and Y. H. Chuang. 2011. 'The Perceived Benefits of Six-degree-separation Social Networks'. *Internet Research* 21, no. 1: 26-45.

Shun, H., C. C. Y. Chen, and Y. S. Jiun. 2006. 'The Application of a Balanced Scorecard in the Performance Evaluation of Higher Education'. *The Total Quality Management Magazine* 18, no. 2: 190-205.

Stemler, S. 2001. 'An Overview of Content Analysis'. *Practical Assessment, Research and Evaluation* 7, no. 17. http://pareonline.net/getvn.asp?v+7&n-17.

Sole, F. 2009. 'A Management Model and Factors Driving Performance in Public Organisations'. *Measuring Business Excellence* 13, no. 4: 3-11.

Verweire, K. and V. L. Van Den Berghe. 2003. 'Integrated Performance Management: Adding a New Dimension'. *Management Decision* 41, no. 8: 782-790.

Weber, R. P. 1990. *Basic Content Analysis*. Newbury Park, CA: Sage.
Winstanley, D. and K. Stuart-Smith. 1996. 'Policing Performance: The Ethics of Performance Management'. *Personnel Review* 25, no. 6: 66-84.
Yin, R. K. 2003. 'Case Study Research, Design and Methods'. *Applied Social Research Methods Series* 5: 79.
Zigan, K., F. Macfarlane, and T. Desombre. 2008. 'Intangible Resources as Performance Drivers in European Hospitals'. *Intangible Journal of Productivity and Performance Management* 57, no. 1: 57-71.

# BOOK REVIEWS

# FROM RECIPIENTS TO DONORS: EMERGING POWERS AND THE CHANGING DEVELOPMENT LANDSCAPE. BY EMMA MAWDSLEY. ZED BOOKS (NEW YORK; LONDON). 2012. 270PP.

In *From Recipients to Donors*, Emma Mawdsley, a Senior Lecturer in the Geography Department at the University of Cambridge, clearly lays out the changing framework of development, looking theoretically, empirically, and analytically at the evolving development landscape. However, for many donor countries, this is not an emergence, but rather a re-emergence. Historically, many of these nations participated in donor and development assistance activities, but the context has changes in a trend towards an increasingly multipolar world. Mawdsley identifies thcse (re-)emerging powers as global powers, such as China, Brazil, and India, but also former socialist states like Russia, Poland, and the Czech Republic; regional powers such as South Africa and Saudi Arabia; and emerging industrial powers like Thailand and Turkey.

Defining terms in a field flooded with options is a challenge, because there are issues with many of these terms: emerging donors, new donors, non-traditional donors, and post-colonial donors all come with exceptions and misrepresentations. Mawdsley therefore labels these (re-)emerging donors as non-DAC donors, or NDD, in reference to the states largely lying outside the Development Assistant Committee (DAC) or the Organisation for Economic Co-operation and Development (OECD). The DAC is made up entirely of Western nations, with the exception of Japan and South Korea, and represents, for Mawdsley, a 'hegemonic' and 'humiliating' model (p. 8).

Mawdsley explains that 'The context for this rapidly changing landscape of aid and development is the seismic shifts taking place in the geographies of power and wealth' (p. 2). Mainstream literature has previously focused on North to South development aid, but, as she points out, researchers are 'increasingly engaging with the rapidly changing map of development actors' (p. 3). Yet it is not just the context that has changed, but also the types of development cooperation. Rather than being the entirety, foreign aid has become just part of the conversation on development.

The world is increasingly turning towards development cooperation and assistance, in a shift from partners to donors. As Mawdsley argues, 'The emergence and/or new visibility of Southern, Gulf and formerly socialist countries as development donors and partners disrupts these persistent Orientalist binaries of North/South, West/East, superior/inferior, donor/recipient' (p. 9). However, she rightly points out that these new partnerships do not come without their problems, and she identifies economic competition, land grabs, environmental and labour issues, and support for oppressive and dictatorial regimes as a few of the challenges these new relationships face.

There are five major themes or arguments that run throughout the course of the book. The first is to move beyond China, a critical point in a literature that has become increasingly China-obsessed. Secondly, she makes an effort to move beyond the empirical and the practices of development assistance to examine 'symbolic politics and development cooperation' (p. 13). The effort is also made to reflect the perspective of the recipient countries and describe their agency in these negotiations. Finally, Mawdsley seeks to critically examine both Western and re-(emerging) donors and development assistance, as well as our understanding of development, broadly speaking.

Chapters one and two provide the foundation for the remainder of the book. In chapter one, Mawdsley lays out the empirical and theoretical framework of her arguments. Specifically, she uses the 'Asian Drivers' framework as the tool for analysing the 'complex impacts' that emerging powers are having on less developed nations. The Asian Drivers framework addresses four key areas of impact - production and trade flows; financial flows; environmental spill overs; and global and regional governance – which are then disaggregated across two axes: direct/indirect and competitive/complementary. Mawdsley argues that 'The Asian Drivers framework is helpful to this analysis of the re-(emerging) development actors because it captures some of the complex dynamics of changing international relations, pointing to plural and heterogeneous impacts for different sectors and social groups within and across different countries and contexts' (p. 22).

In chapter two, she takes an important step back into history, explaining that in fact many of these forms of development cooperation are not new. She briefly lays out the historical lineage of socialist development aid, as well as development cooperation within the Non-Alignment Movement and the United Nations South-South Cooperation initiatives. She also examines the impact of the rise of oil prices and the global economic downturn in the 1970s, as well as the creation and expansion of the European Union. While each of the five major historical lineages Mawdsley identifies are only discussed in brief, their import is undeniable and points the way forward for further historically based studies on development cooperation in the future.

Chapters 3 to 7 discuss the contemporary era, focusing on the 21st century. Chapter 3 lays out the facts and figures of NDD assistance, including institutions, recipients, and flows. Chapter 4 takes these figures a step further, discussing the modalities and practices of these development partnerships. Chapter 5 shifts the discussion to examine the discourse surrounding NDDs. How these relationships are constructed, by those giving and those receiving, as well as those observing from the outside, is a crucial point of analysis. Mawdsley takes this a step further, looking at the relationship between foreign aid and national identity. Critically, here, and elsewhere throughout the book, she emphasises 'the importance of historical and contemporary specificity' (p. 146). Examples are just that, and the complexity cannot be fully expressed by the totality.

In chapter 6, Mawdsley addresses this challenge through a discussion on global governance, asking, how can foreign aid and development cooperation be governed? Here, she highlights the major themes of credibility, legitimacy, and incentives, as well as laying out from which institutions these issues are being governed - including a discussion of the World Bank, the International Monetary Fund, the OECD-DAC, the UN Development Cooperation Forum, and the G20. Finally, in chapter 7, the conclusion, Mawdsley examines the movement from aid to development 'effectiveness' (p. 209). Here she discusses the Working Party on Aid Effectiveness, which points to the future of development partnerships.

Overall, the book is an excellent overview of the changing development landscape. However, as Mawdsley also points out herself, there is the need for further analysis on each of these issues. Specialists may find the book too broad based, but it is a great text for students and policy makers, particularly due to its attention to the long history of development cooperation. The analysis is largely focused on state actors, but there are references to non-state actors, giving the book a wider interdisciplinary appeal. It is well written and organised, clearly argued, and the side box case studies make it particularly useful for classroom instruction. It is, in sum, an important addition to the literature on development.

Jessica Achberger
Southern African Institute for Policy and Research

# SCRAMBLE FOR AFRICA: FROM THE OLD WORLD TO THE NEW. BY HARRY STEPHAN AND MICHAEL POWER. RENAISSANCE PRESS (CAPE TOWN), 2012. 454PP.

Harry Stephan and Michael Power's latest book, *Scramble for Africa: From the Old World to the New*, is a must read for students of African development, political science, and international relations. The book describes about how Africa can reap the benefits of the rise of China in the new global economy. It uses the framework of realism and international political economy theories of power and wealth to explain the current global political state and why Africa has a second chance at development. Africa has a chance to be freed from the bondage of commodity extraction, marginalization, and existence within the periphery in the new global economy necessitated by the rise of China.

Robert Shrire, Professor of International Relations at University of Cape Town, in his foreword notes that Stephan and Power bring with them academic acumen and experience in business to argue their case for African development. Shrire notes that the book fills the gap between theories of international political economy and the challenges of African economic development. Stephan, in the introductory chapter, asks the primary question the book addresses: where is Africa going? The remaining five chapters of the book offer us a prognosis and a prediction of where Africa ought to be in the twenty-first century. Power's two chapters, chapter two and chapter three, take the reader to the level of the firm in understanding capital, product life cycle, and the economic hierarchy of states. This analysis further leads us to a description of why and how nation states have attracted capital. It specifically argues why China's rise and engagement with Africa is beyond commodity extraction.

Chapter four, by Raymond Steenkamp, tackles the post-World War II regime under the Bretton Woods institutions and the ideology of free trade. He walks us through the General Agreement on Tariffs and Trade

(GATT) and the World Trade Organisation (WTO), focusing primarily on how and why Africa was marginalised in these processes. He argues that western countries have failed to follow the dictates of comparative advantage as preached by David Ricardo. Steenkamp further brings out the relevance of the BRICS (Brazil, Russia, India, China, and South Africa) countries in south-to-south trade.

In chapter five, Stephan and Bridgman argue the case for globalisation, regime theory, and what China brings to the fore. Rochela and Angus then bring the reader back home with their analysis of the Southern African Development Community (SADC) and broader regionalism in Africa. Where do South African foreign policy, SADC, and the New Economic Partnership for African Development (NEPAD) fit in to this question of African development in the twenty-first century? Will the key variables: African elites, the land question, and trade combine to get the best outcome from the current state of geopolitics?

Harry Stephan's work has all the questions that demand investigation. Have the African leaders and the African people really decided where they want to go? Stephan argues that Africa is moving from the old world to the new world. He traces Africa's old world through three great scholars: William Wilberforce, Karl Polanyi, and Franz Fanon. A quick glance at the contribution of these scholars demonstrates Africa's quest for integration in the global capitalist system. However, the question that begs to be answered is: who are Africa's scholars in the new world?

I believe this series will stand alongside the giants of Fanon, Polanyi, and Wilberforce in telling the complete story of Africa. However, African pessimists will find this book a hard read. Conclusions and predictions that come from this analysis are startling and defy pedestrian conclusions. A quick glance at the continent still shows a proliferation of NGOs providing service delivery against the background of a demonised/vilified state; a continent laden with autocratic old leaders clinging to power; and a continent ravaged by poverty, hunger, disease. Therefore, this book makes an excellent text for African elites, government officials, businessmen, scholars, and students. Fundamental questions must be asked now and answered correctly for Africa to claim the twenty-first century.

Lawrence Michelo
Independent Researcher

# THE COLLAPSE OF RHODESIA: POPULATION DEMOGRAPHICS AND THE POLITICS OF RACE. BY JOSIAH BROWNELL. I. B. TAURUS (LONDON, UK). 2011. 241PP.

From its establishment as a colony in 1890, Southern Rhodesia, later called Rhodesia and now Zimbabwe, has attracted a considerable amount of scholarship. Scholars have contributed immensely to the extension of the frontiers of Rhodesian history and historiography. The issues discussed range from the occupation of the country, fortune hunting, mining, and politics, to the seizure of land, the role of settler farmers, and race relations. This study, by Josiah Brownell, is a controversial re-examination of racial population demographics, looking at the basic components of population growth and change, fertility, and mortality among Europeans and Africans, as well as Indians and coloureds. These parameters varied in detail from one race to another and highlight the importance of racial demographics and their impact on the role of the state, policy formulation, land and other economic issues, politics, and, most importantly, on how differing numbers in each race dictated the issues of the day. The appearance of *The Collapse of Rhodesia* is most welcome, because, for the first time, the issue of government efforts to secure demographic factors has been highlighted as an important factor in the politics of Rhodesia, leading to the Unilateral Declaration of Independence (UDI) in 1965.

The author sees the Rhodesian State as a 'unique' species unto itself that straddled the 'legal and conceptual definitions' of what it was to be a settler state (179). It was not only a settler colony on the path to independence under a white regime, but also a colony destined for indigenous rule, 'without exactly fitting into either one' (179). The settler farmers formed what Godfrey Higgins, the former Prime Minister of Southern Rhodesia, called 'white islands in a black sea' (994), to imply and indicate their isolation. In all these discussions, the issues of contest for political power, economic dominance, and race relations have been discussed at varying depths. There were concerted efforts by the State to stabilise the population of the Europeans and 'restore' whiter settler confidence. The greatest fear was the emerging picture of migration losses as this decreased the number of settlers, their influence, and their political clout (2).

Brownell argues that the story of Rhodesia between 1960 and 1979 was a 'war of numbers', providing 'insights into the fundamental nature of both white settler society and the settler state which are missed in more orthodox narratives' (7). The State 'attempted' to discover the contours of the demography of Rhodesia by conducting censuses. The population numbers helped the State to address racial imbalances, and it used these numbers in different ways for different purposes. The numbers were at times weapons used against enemies; they also provided a pretext for taking certain actions that were desired or seen to be necessary. The numbers could be used to boost popularity as a sign of the success of the policies. At times, when these numbers were seen to be negative for the State, they were not disclosed. As such, Brownell argues that the counting of people in different categories and the control over population statistics were extremely important for the Rhodesian State to control, rationalise, regulate, and manipulate the population numbers and the demographic factors that drove them, as well as examine the accompanying and prevailing attitudes of the Rhodesian settler population (25-26). Brownell adds that 'the war of numbers' was between the rate of natural increase among the Africans and the rate of net migration by the Europeans, which was the greatest source of growth. It was waged both by the State, dominated by white settlers (97-130), and the African nationalists who were seeking to dislodge them (131-164). The 'war' was primarily political, but it had obvious military and diplomatic components, as well as social and cultural aspects (165-169).

Using Albert O. Hirschman's theory of exit, voice, and loyalty, Brownell argues that in the colonial history of Southern Rhodesia, the settler state was unable to attract and retain a sizeable or stable European population (76-79). A large number of Europeans remained 'transients', with one foot in the country when things were going well for them and the other out to leave as soon as things proved to be bad. This situation developed in spite of the aggressive efforts made to secure a sizable European population. The growth of the population remained low, hovering around 5% from 1955 to 1961 and dropping to 3% in 1980. On the other hand, the African population remained in a majority. The State saw a solution in increasing white immigration, which was seen as a 'panacea' to cure the political and economic ills because it would increase the overall white population and raise their morale. A reduction in numbers was seen as an indication of failure (130).

In the past these issues were not linked to the demographic and racial patterns and their influence on politics in Rhodesia. Brownell has scored a first in critically analysing the vital demographic components that buttressed the multifaceted conflicts in Rhodesia before 1980. *The Collapse of Rhodesia* is the first book that has addressed the importance of demography in Southern Africa and is an important contribution to the historiography of Rhodesia. The most important contribution is the author's critical analysis, which shows that the disparity in demography between the Europeans and Africans was an important factor in the political developments in Rhodesia. The same thesis could also be applied to the situation in Kenya, the southern part of Nyasaland, the Eastern and Southern parts of Northern Rhodesia, South Africa, and Namibia. The author shows that censuses did more than just count people. The numbers they produced indicated a variety of political and economic impacts, demonstrating domination and marginalisation.

As someone who has taught studies of land and labour in Malawi, Zambia, and Zimbabwe for many years, in which populations figures played a major part in the analysis of racial disparity, domination, land dispossession of Africans, forced labour, and poor conditions of service, I find this study most informative and instructive on the current racial disparities in Zimbabwe. I recommend the book very highly.

Mwelwa C. Musambachime
University of Zambia

# Zambia Social Science Journal

Call for Papers

The *Zambia Social Science Journal* is an interdisciplinary, peer-reviewed journal published by the Southern African Institute for Policy and Research. The primary objective is to publish scholarly work in the social sciences and development. Serving as a forum for argument, debate, review, reflection, and discussion, the Journal is informed by the results of relevant and rigorous research. Articles are welcome from scholars and researchers at all career stages from within and outside Africa. Articles from any field within the social sciences relevant to Africa may be submitted.

The published papers are anonymously peer reviewed by at least three reviewers. Final acceptance or rejection of submitted papers rests with the Editorial Board. The Editorial Board reserves the right to refuse any material for publication. The Journal is published bi-annually, with editions coming out in May and November.

Submission guidelines can be found on the SAIPAR website, www.saipar.org.